About the Author

Gerald Dickens is a great-great-grandson of Charles Dickens and has been performing one-man stage shows based on the life and works of his ancestor for over twenty years, undertaking major tours of both the UK and America each year. As part of his performance of the atmospheric ghost story *The Signalman* Gerald began to research the circumstances behind the Staplehurst rail disaster which led to the writing of this book.

He lives in Abingdon with his wife and youngest children.

Dickens and Staplehurst
A Biography of a Rail Crash

Gerald Dickens

Dickens and Staplehurst
A Biography of a Rail Crash

Olympia Publishers
London

www.olympiapublishers.com
OLYMPIA PAPERBACK EDITION

A CIP catalogue record for this title is
available from the British Library.

ISBN: 978-1-78830-851-9

This is a work of creative nonfiction. The events are portrayed to the
best of the author's memory. While all the stories in this book are
true, some names and identifying details have been changed to
protect the privacy of the people involved.

First Published in 2021

Olympia Publishers
Tallis House
2 Tallis Street
London
EC4Y 0AB

Printed in Great Britain

Dedication

To Liz, Cameron, Lily and Layla

And

The Victims of Staplehurst

Emma Beaumont
Annie Bodenham
Hannah Condliff
James Dunn
Charlotte Faithful
Adam Hampson
Hippolite Mercier
Amelia Rayner
Lydia Whitby
Caroline White

Acknowledgements

I am indebted to many people who have assisted me in putting this book together and in no particular order I thank them for their time, expertise and generosity:

In memory of Janine Watrin who showed me Boulogne, put up with my woeful French and shared her encyclopaedic knowledge of Charles Dickens with me;
Archives Municipales, Boulogne;
Kevin Dare and the volunteers at The Didcot Railway Centre for telling me all about steam trains and allowing me on the footplate to drive one;
Lorna Standen from the Hereford archives for bringing the Bodenham family to life;
Alan Taylor from Folkestone for his invaluable knowledge of the cross-channel boat and rail services.
Cindy Sughrue and her staff at The Charles Dickens Museum;
Professor Nicholas Cambridge.
Mark Tyrrell for helping me to understand the symptoms and consequences of Post-Traumatic Stress Disorder;
Peter Redfern.

INTRODUCTION

This book is a biography of a single day: June 9th, 1865. For many years I have been performing a one-man stage show based on Charles Dickens' haunting ghost story *The Signalman*. By way of introduction, I relate the story of Dickens' involvement in the Staplehurst rail crash which took place just over a year before he wrote the tale, and no doubt influenced it. Over time I began to get interested in the story behind the crash, wanting to know what actually happened rather than just regurgitating the few rather sensational facts which I had gleaned from the various biographies of Dickens that rarely give the incident more than a few paragraphs.

My search began one day when I found the Board of Trade report into the crash and suddenly, I had names: the driver George Crombie, the Foreman of Platelayers Henry Benge, and a few others, made the whole scene become a little more real. My interested piqued, I searched more deeply and eventually found the formal entries of death for the victims, and it was then as I saw their names for the first time that I knew I had to tell their story. Here were ten individuals whose identities had been forgotten thanks to the fact that Charles Dickens, my great-great-grandfather, happened to have been on the same train, on the same day as them.

Dickens was a great letter writer, so my next step was to read all of his correspondence from the summer of 1865 and in the midst of it all I found one letter mentioning that the article in *The Examiner* had stated the facts of the accident correctly, so my research took me into the wonderful world of the UK Newspaper Archive which holds copies of almost every newspaper (national and regional) from every day, dating back to the 1700s, and it was then that the whole story began to unfold before my eyes. Naturally, thanks to the celebrity involved, the press was ravenous for facts and the many journalists printed everything that they could find about everyone involved, leaving me with the job, 155 years later, of collating and retelling the entire story.

As part of my research, I travelled to the site of the crash, just outside Staplehurst, and ignoring padlocked gates and notices telling me that this was 'Private Property' I followed the railway track until I reached the low bridge that crosses the River Beult. I had ten red roses with me that I wanted to lay at the scene in memory of the victims and the presence of a perfect rainbow seemed to bring affirmation to my trespassing. It was a November day and the river had flooded the fields and the little copse of trees which nestle close to the bridge. I wanted to get nearer, so stepped into an innocuous looking puddle among the trees, but it was deeper than I expected, and my boot continued down until the muddy water flooded over the top. I uttered an expletive which probably wasn't respectful, and tried to pull my step back, at which point the ground began to give way and my foot slipped down the slimy mud bank until I found myself up to my neck in cold water.

And it was at that moment, more than studying documents and letters, that what transpired on the 9th June, 1865 became real to me and for an instant I felt a complete affinity with the passengers of the tidal train which ended its journey at exactly the same spot.

Sources

I am also grateful to those who have researched and written before me and whose work I have been able to use to steer me in the right direction.

In particular I must credit Claire Tomalin and her remarkable biography of Ellen Ternan: *The Invisible Woman*. Her investigative research was remarkable and most of our knowledge of Ellen comes from her.

I also credit the following as being valuable source material:

The Letters of Charles Dickens 1820-1870, The British Newspaper Archive

The Life of Charles Dickens by John Forster

Charles Dickens: A Life by Claire Tomalin

Charles Dickens by Michael Slater

Dickens: A Biography by Fred Kaplan

Dickens by Peter Ackroyd

Charles Dickens by Edgar Johnson

Charles Dickens & M. Beaucourt-Mutuel: The History of a Friendship by Janine Watrin

Charles Dickens and his Performing Selves by Malcolm Andrews

Charles Dickens by his Eldest Daughter by Mamie Dickens

Dickens' Artistic Daughter, Katey by Lucinda Hawksley

Memories of my Father as I Recall Him by Mamie Dickens

Memories of my Father by Sir Henry F Dickens

Charles Dickens as I Knew Him by George Dolby

Red for Danger by LTC Rolt

Boat Trains & Channel Packets by Rixon Bucknall

The History of the South Eastern Railway by George Angus Nokes

PROLOGUE

The June day was a hot one, and the early summer sun shone brightly from a clear blue sky. On the footplate of locomotive number 199 nothing seemed to be amiss; the express tidal train was maintaining a steady 50 miles per hour as it rushed across the Kentish countryside towards London. The hand on the regulator lever was that of George Crombie, a man of great experience with the South Eastern Railway Company and a careful driver. There was little for him to do, for the track was straight and flat and his view ahead was clear, although slightly hindered by the low afternoon sun to his left.

With him in the cab was his fireman William Beattie, who apart from shovelling coal into the roaring furnace was also keeping a professional watch on the water gauges in order to ensure that there was always a constant pressure at the boiler. Elsewhere on the train other employees of the railway company maintained their lonely vigils in their dark guards' vans, with no duties to occupy their time.

Behind the locomotive there were eleven passenger carriages, and these were filled by a cast of characters most of whom had risen early in Paris that morning in order to join the train to Boulogne where they would board the steamer Victoria to Folkestone. The regular cross channel service was a popular one and the service on June 9th had around 110 passengers all bound for London. There were businessmen travelling alone, there were mothers with children returning from a trip to rejoin the rest of their families. There were elderly couples who had taken the opportunity of joining a sight-seeing excursion to Paris. There was a French chef returning to Plymouth where he was in the employ of a British admiral, although he had allowed himself a few days in London to meet up with his friends before heading West.

In the first of the first-class carriages sat a gentleman and two ladies, each lost in their own thoughts. The gentleman studied a sheaf of handwritten papers and occasionally a smile, maybe a chuckle, broke his lips. His bright eyes shone with great intensity. He was accompanied by two ladies, a younger one of 26 who sat next to him and her mother sitting opposite.'There was an intensity to them too, although at that moment they were not in the same world as their companion. The man was Charles Dickens and he travelled with his mistress Ellen Ternan and her mother Frances.

At Headcorn station the buildings flashed by in a rush and perhaps some of the children on the train gasped in shock at the sudden change in noise and light. Their parents held them close, laughed and reassured them — everything was perfectly alright, they were quite safe. The uninformed assumption from the carriages was officially confirmed on the footplate, for Crombie noticed that the signals were set to 'All Clear'. The train sped on.

And then it happened. A whistle, two whistles. A lurching as brakes were applied, a huge noise as the great driving wheels were reversed. The carriages shuddered. Charles Dickens, Ellen and Frances were flung from their seats into the corner of the compartment. A moment before, everything had been ordered and clear, and now all was confusion: the wall became the roof and the roof the wall. Ellen lay at the bottom of the human heap with her arm twisted to an unnatural angle and she cried out to Dickens to hold her hand.

For a moment all was quiet, and then the screaming began.

It was 3.20 PM on Friday 9th June, 1865 and the remains of the tidal train lay shattered in the river Beult near to the Wealden town of Staplehurst. This is the story of how Charles Dickens, Ellen Ternan and the rest of the passengers came to be involved in one of the most serious rail disasters of the day.

In the following pages I will explain how Charles Dickens rose to become one of the greatest celebrities of the Victorian era and how he came to be travelling on the ill-fated train with Ellen and Frances Ternan. I will show how a routine repair to the railway line led to disaster, and the overlooking of numerous failsafes demanded by the regulations exacerbated the situation. I will describe the terror at the scene of the crash and Charles Dickens' involvement in the rescue of his fellow passengers, as well as his suffering in the days, weeks and years following the accident.

At its heart this is a story of a single moment in time: a biography of a day.

A Perfectly Ordinary Day. 9th June, 1865

Charles Dickens and his dog Turk. 1865

The 9th June, 1865 was a perfectly ordinary day in a perfectly ordinary summer. The morning newspapers reported a debate in Parliament over the expansion of the National Gallery and there was much delighting in the fact that the collection was not to be moved from the Trafalgar Square site and indeed the land occupied by the parish workhouse situated behind the current building would be purchased and utilised. In a remarkable show of cross-party support '...the house showed its confidence in the wisdom and economy of government by voting whatever was asked for.'

The Madame Tussaud Exhibition in Baker Street announced that they would be displaying a full-length model of President Lincoln, and another of John Wilkes Booth 'the reputed assassin of the late President Lincoln, taken from a likeness presented by himself to Mrs Stratton, wife of General Tom Thumb'.

The Court Circular column of the *Morning Advertiser* reported from Balmoral that the Queen had driven out, accompanied by Princess Louise. A bulletin from Marlborough House reassured the public that 'Her Royal Highness, the Princess of Wales is steadily advancing towards recovery' and that 'the infant Prince continues well'. The Prince referred to had been born on 3rd June and would later become George V.

The Prince of Wales meanwhile had visited Lord's cricket ground where he watched The Household Brigade play I Zingari. The match was played over a single innings. The Brigade batted first and amassed 217 which was enough for them to emerge victorious despite some 'fine batting' by Mr Buller for I Zingari, scoring 61 runs for his team.

The death was announced of Joseph Paxton who had found fame designing the great Crystal Palace which had formed the centrepiece at The Great Exhibition of 1851. Paxton was a friend of Charles Dickens and his famous design would influence the conservatory that would be the 'final improvement' at Gad's Hill Place, Dickens' country home in Kent.

From Brentwood in Essex there was a report about 'one of the most successful stock and agricultural shows we ever remember in the county'. The article went on to praise the organisation of the event mentioning that 'the committee had devoted a goodly sum to the decorations of the town, that nothing might be wanting in the outward signs of welcome to the society, and in the gaiety of the holiday garb of the town for the visitors'.

On a more mournful note, there were many lurid accounts of the awful rail crash that had occurred at Rednal, near Oswestry in Shropshire, and which had claimed the lives of eleven people, injuring many more.

June 9th was an ordinary morning, but for ten people it would be the last one that they would ever know, and for others their lives were destined to change forever.

PART ONE:
DICKENS AND TERNAN

The Early Life of Charles Dickens

By the summer of 1865 Charles Dickens was one of the most famous and recognisable people in Britain, if not the world. For thirty years he had not only been delighting his readers with his novels but he had also become a spokesman for a generation, a man who understood the poor and downtrodden and who brought their struggles and their plight firmly into the public eye and demanded that action be taken on their behalf.

Charles Dickens had burst upon the literary scene in 1836 when, writing under the pseudonym Boz, he had submitted a series of stories about everyday life to *The Monthly Magazine* published in London. These stories, or sketches as he called them, bore the hallmarks that would become the standard for popular literature over the coming years: the scenes were described with an exquisite detail and the characters larger than life whilst remaining absolutely believable. Much of what he wrote was centred around the streets of London that he had known as a child.

Dickens had been born in the naval port of Portsmouth on the south coast of England, not because the family had any roots there but because his father was working at the Royal Dockyards as a pay clerk. It has been suggested, probably erroneously but certainly romantically, that Charles's parents were dancing a jig the night before his birth, thereby bringing into the world a baby imbued with the desire to entertain.

Being duty-bound to the Royal Navy John Dickens was frequently moved on, and the family left Portsmouth before Charles was a year old, firstly settling in London and then in Kent where the little boy would enjoy the happiest years of his childhood. The family lived in Chatham on the banks of the River Medway where many of the great warships had been built, including the *Victory* that had been the flagship of Admiral Lord Nelson at the battle of Trafalgar in 1805 and which was the pride of a nation.

As a boy Charles roamed the fields and countryside around Chatham and the experiences filled his mind with vivid scenes that would never leave him. Much of his later writing was firmly based around the conjoined towns of Chatham and Rochester. In *The Uncommercial Traveller* published in 1860 he wrote of his childhood memories in the essay 'Dullborough Town':

'Of course, the town had shrunk fearfully, since I was a child there. I had entertained the impression that the High-street was at least as wide as Regent-street, London, or the Italian Boulevard at Paris. I found it little better than a lane. There was a public clock in it, which I had supposed to be the finest clock in the world: whereas it now turned out to be as inexpressive, moon-faced, and weak a clock as ever I saw. It belonged to a Town Hall, where I had seen an Indian (who I now suppose wasn't an Indian) swallow a sword (which I now suppose he didn't). The edifice had appeared to me in those days so glorious a structure, that I had set it up in my mind as the model on which the Genie of the Lamp built the palace for Aladdin. A mean little brick heap, like a demented chapel, with a few yawning persons in leather gaiters, and in the last extremity for something to do, lounging at the door with their hands in their pockets, and calling themselves a Corn Exchange!

'The Theatre was in existence, I found, on asking the fishmonger, who had a compact show of stock in his window, consisting of a sole and a quart of shrimps — and I resolved to comfort my mind by going to look at it. Richard the Third, in a very uncomfortable cloak, had first appeared to me there, and had made my heart leap with terror by backing up against the stage-box in which I was posted, while struggling for life against the virtuous Richmond. It was within those walls that I had learnt as from a page of English history, how that wicked King slept in war-time on a sofa much too short for him, and how fearfully his conscience troubled his boots.

'Many wondrous secrets of Nature had I come to the knowledge of in that sanctuary: of which not the least terrific were that the witches in *Macbeth* bore an awful resemblance to the Thanes and other proper inhabitants of Scotland; and that the good King Duncan couldn't rest in his grave, but was constantly coming out of it and calling himself somebody else. To the Theatre, therefore, I repaired for consolation. But I found very little, for it was in a bad and declining way. A dealer in wine and bottled beer had already squeezed his trade into the box-office, and the theatrical money was taken — when it came — in a kind of meat-safe in the passage. The dealer in wine and bottled beer must have insinuated himself under the stage too; for he announced that he had various descriptions of alcoholic drinks 'in the wood', and there was no possible stowage for the wood anywhere else. Evidently, he was by degrees eating the establishment away to the core, and would soon have sole possession of it. It was To Let, and hopelessly so, for its old purposes; and there had been no entertainment within its walls for a long time except a Panorama; and even that had been announced as 'pleasingly instructive', and I know too well the fatal meaning and the leaden import of those terrible expressions. No, there was no comfort in the Theatre. It was mysteriously gone, like my own youth. Unlike my own youth, it might be coming back some day; but there was little promise of it.'

Kent and the countryside surrounding the River Medway would remain Dickens' constant companions throughout his career, both physically and in his literature; *The Pickwick Papers*, *Oliver Twist*, *David Copperfield*, *Great Expectations*, *A Tale of Two Cities*, *The Mystery of Edwin Drood* would all feature the county among their pages.

When Charles was ten years old John Dickens was relocated to London once more and the family found their home in a small house in Camden Town, where the Cratchit family would also live twenty years later.

The open fields and endless countryside of Chatham were now but distant memories, for Charles Dickens was entering a dark period of his life which would torment him for evermore. John Dickens lived an improvident lifestyle which pulled the family further and further into debt until eventually he was arrested and imprisoned at the Marshalsea Debtors' Prison located to the south of the River Thames in Southwark.

Charles, now twelve, was sent to work in an attempt to raise the money to support his family and to clear the debt, his place of employment being a factory producing shoe blacking owned by Mr Warren. It was situated at Old Hungerford Stairs, close to the spot where Charing Cross station would later be built, where the injured victims of the Staplehurst rail crash would be brought and cared for.

The shame of his time at Warren's Blacking, and the fact that his father was a convicted debtor, never left Charles, and he wouldn't speak of it to his family during his lifetime. For a man who would go on to live an extravagant life among the high society of London the pain was almost unbearable, and it is no surprise that he attempted to exorcise those memories by releasing them into his work. The most obvious attempt to do this was in *David Copperfield* during which the titular character is sent to work at Murdstone and Grinby's bottling factory, located at Hungerford Stairs.

'Murdstone and Grinby's trade was among a good many kind of people, but an important branch of it was the supply of wines and spirits to certain packet ships. I forget now where they chiefly went, but I think there were some among them that made voyages both to the East and West Indies. I know that a great many empty bottles were one of the consequences of this traffic, and that certain men and boys were employed to examine them against the light, and reject those that were flawed, and to rinse and wash them. When the empty bottles ran short, there were labels to be pasted on full ones, or corks to be fitted to them, or seals to be put upon the corks, or finished bottles to be packed in casks. All this work was my work, and of the boys employed upon it I was one…'

'The deep remembrance of the sense I had, of being utterly without hope now; of the shame I felt in my position; of the misery it was to my young heart to believe that day by day what I had learned, and thought, and delighted in, and raised my fancy and my emulation up by, would pass away from me, little by little, never to be brought back any more; cannot be written.'

Not only is David sent to work labelling bottles but the

nearest thing he has to a father figure in London, Wilkins Micawber, lives a feckless existence which sees him imprisoned until his debts can be paid off. Charles even gives the hero of the story his own initials, albeit reversed.

Much of the detail of Charles's childhood may have remained a mystery, a puzzle within the pages of literature to be solved only by a curious and eagle-eyed biographer, were it not for what is known as 'the autobiographical fragment', a sort of confession, if you like, that Charles made to John Forster, his close, trusted friend and the author of the first biography which would be published three years after his death. This is what Charles told him:

'...In an evil hour for me, as I often bitterly thought. Its chief manager, James Lambert, the relative who had lived with us in Bayham Street, seeing how I was employed from day to day, and knowing what our domestic circumstances then were, proposed that I should go into the blacking warehouse, to be as useful as I could, at a salary, I think, of six shillings a week. I am not clear whether it was six or seven, I am inclined to believe, from my uncertainty on this head, that it was six at first, and seven afterwards. At any rate, the offer was accepted very willingly by my mother, and on a Monday morning I went down to the blacking warehouse to begin my business life.

'It is wonderful to me how I could have so easily been cast away at such an early age. It is wonderful to me that, even after my descent into the poor little drudge I had been since we came to London, no one had compassion enough on me — a child of singular abilities: quick, eager, delicate, and soon hurt, bodily or mentally — to suggest that something might have been spared, as certainly it might have been, to place me at any common school.

'The blacking warehouse was the last house on the left-hand side of the way at Old Hungerford Stairs. It was a crazy, tumbledown old house, abutting of course on the river, and literally overrun with rats. Its wainscoted rooms and its rotten floors and staircase, and the old grey rats swarming down in the cellars, and the sound of their squeaking and scuffling coming up the stairs at all times, and the dirt and decay of the place, rise up visibly before me, as if I were there again. The counting house was on the first floor, looking over the coal-barges and the river. There was a recess in it, in which I was to sit and work.

'My work was to cover the pots of paste-blacking: first with a piece of oil-paper, and then with a piece of blue paper, to tie them round with a string; and then to clip the paper close and neat all round, until it looked as smart as a pot of ointment from an apothecary's shop. When a certain number of grosses of pots had attained this pitch of perfection I was to paste on each printed label; and then go on again with more pots.

'Two or three other boys were kept at similar duty downstairs on similar wages. One of them came up, in a ragged apron, to show me the trick of using the string and tying the knot. His name was Bob Fagin; and I took the liberty of using his name, long afterwards, in Oliver Twist.'

Every day after toiling in the warehouse Charles walked across the river to visit his father in the Marshalsea, as would Little Dorrit in the novel of the same name.

Eventually the little frail child was released from his position thanks to a small inheritance left to the family by a relation of his mother's, but the psychological damage had been done and the circumstances of that time of his life would haunt Charles Dickens forever.

The Charles Dickens that emerged from Warren's Blacking was not only a damaged one but also a strengthened one: his spirit was strong, and he was determined never to allow himself or his family to descend so low again. Whatever life held he would embrace it firmly and make the most of every situation; simply, he decided, he would be the best at everything he undertook.

Despite a short spell at Wellington Academy (which establishment Dickens was horrified to discover had been razed to the ground to make way for a new railway when he visited the spot with his biographer John Forster towards the end of his life), Charles received little formal education but he loved to read and would devour adventure stories. His ability to become completely wrapped up in a scene is beautifully illustrated in *A Christmas Carol*, when Ebenezer Scrooge is shown a vison of himself as a child reading, and the images from the page envelop him. For the first time in the book the old miser is excited, and the words tumble from him:

'"Why, it's Ali Baba." Scrooge exclaimed in extasy. "It's dear old honest Ali Baba. Yes, yes, I know. One Christmas time, when yonder solitary child was left here all alone, he did come, for the first time, just like that. Poor Boy. And Valentine," said Scrooge, "and his wild brother, Orson; there they go.

'"And what's his name, who was put down in his drawers, asleep, at the Gate of Damascus; don't you see him. And the Sultan's Groom turned upside down by the Genii; there he is upon his head. Serve him right. I'm glad of it. What business had he to be married to the Princess."

'To hear Scrooge expending all the earnestness of his nature on such subjects, in a most extraordinary voice would have been a surprise to his business friends in the city, indeed.

"'There's the parrot.'" Cried Scrooge. "Green body and yellow tail, with a thing like a lettuce growing out of the top of his head; there he is. Poor Robinson Crusoe, he called him when he came home again after sailing round the island. 'Poor Robinson Crusoe, where have you been, Robinson Crusoe?' The man thought he was dreaming, but he wasn't. It was the parrot, you know. There goes Friday, running for his life to the little creek. Halloa. Hoop. Hallo!'"

Among Charles's favourite books was *The Adventures of Roderick Random* written by Tobias Smollet in 1748. The book is a naval adventure set on the high seas in which the hero makes his way through a plotless story becoming involved in a series of exciting escapades surrounded by some wonderful characters who continually return throughout the narrative. Along the way Smollet was able to expose the greed and hypocrisy of the establishment (in this case the Royal Navy), and champion the cause of the underdog: it was a model that would serve Charles Dickens very well in his own writing career.

The love of storytelling meant that Charles Dickens was always destined to be a communicator and after a short spell as a legal clerk, working at the chambers of Ellis and Blackmore's in Gray's Inn, he inevitably was drawn towards journalism. John Dickens was already a parliamentary journalist at *The Morning Chronicle* and in a bid to emulate his father Charles embarked on the not inconsiderable task of teaching himself shorthand, and further educated himself by spending long hours in the reading room at The British Museum.

After two years spent as a peripatetic journalist reporting on the tedious and mundane proceedings of Doctors' Commons Charles finally entered the gallery (meaning that he was able to report from the press gallery in the Houses of Parliament) at the age of nineteen years old. He initially worked for *The True Sun* newspaper, then *The Mirror of Parliament* until at last he joined his father at *The Morning Chronicle*. Another young journalist on the staff remembered seeing 'a young man of my own age whose keen animation of look would have arrested attention anywhere, and whose name, upon inquiry, I then for the first time heard'. That journalist was John Forster, to whom, as we have seen, Dickens would share the secret of his childhood so many years later. On the occasion of their first meeting Dickens had been standing up for his fellow journalists at *The Morning Chronicle* who were involved in a strike; even at the age of nineteen Charles Dickens was championing the case of the underdogs.

It was a fine time to be a political journalist, for the Great Reform Bill was being debated, meaning that every newspaper needed reporters in great numbers so that every word could be recorded. Dickens spent days, weeks and months in the house listening to the debates and ensuring that he recorded them accurately. Such were his long hours and levels of concentration that he completely exhausted himself, on one occasion writing to a friend apologising for missing an appointment saying that 'I was so exceedingly tired from my week's exertions that I slept on the sofa the whole day'.

During 1833 Charles had begun to write short stories of London life, observations written with a journalist's eye for detail, and during the autumn of that year he decided to submit one of them anonymously to a publication called *The Monthly Magazine*. Remembering his first foray into the world of literature Dickens would recall many years later that the manuscript had been 'dropped stealthily one evening at twilight, with fear and trembling, into a dark letter-box, in a dark office up a dark court in Fleet Street'.

The Monthly Magazine saw potential in the story and published it in the December edition. Of course the author couldn't be informed, as none of the editorial staff knew who he was, so it was with a sense of surprise and extreme pride that Charles Dickens purchased a copy from a bookstall on The Strand and read: 'Mr. Augustus Minns was a bachelor, of about forty as he said — of about eight-and-forty as his friends said. He was always exceedingly clean, precise, and tidy; perhaps somewhat priggish, and the most retiring man in the world.'

The literary career of Charles Dickens had begun.

The Monthly Magazine was interested in more of the sketches, as they came to be known, and published them regularly throughout the following year initially without a by-line, until August of '34 Dickens began to use the pen-name Boz, a nickname of his youngest brother Augustus 'whom,' explained Forster 'in honour of the *Vicar of Wakefield* he had dubbed Moses, which being facetiously pronounced through the nose became Boses, and being shortened became Boz'. The writings of the older Boz became extremely popular with the readers and soon they were being spoken of in coffee houses and clubs across the city. Eventually Charles was approached by the editor of a new venture, *The Evening Chronicle*, which was to be an offshoot of *The Morning Chronicle* for whom he was still working as a journalist. The editor asked if a new sketch could be written especially for the first edition and Dickens agreed, providing there was suitable remuneration involved (he had not been paid for his *Monthly Magazine* contributions). His regular salary of five guineas was increased to seven and the agreement was finalised. The editor of the *Evening Chronicle* was George Hogarth who had a daughter named Catherine.

Catherine and Charles were soon engaged, the young journalist to the editor's daughter, and they were married on April 2 1836, honeymooning in the Kentish village of Chalk, close to the hills and fields in which he had played so happily just a few years before.

1836 was to be a busy year for Charles Dickens for not only was there his wedding to celebrate but the sketches were collected and published in two volumes imaginatively entitled *Sketches by Boz*.

Further to those developments Dickens was also approached by the publishing house of Chapman and Hall with a proposal for an all new project in association with a popular artist of the day, Robert Seymour. The plan was for Seymour to create a series of comical prints showing the members of a sporting club getting into all sorts of difficulties 'for want of dexterity' and Charles would be required to provide witty text to accompany them. The club would be called 'The Nimrod Club'.

For a recently married young man the proposal was appealing, but Charles believed that the project would be more effective with a few changes. Firstly, Dickens argued, he had no great knowledge of sports, so a wider subject matter would make more sense; anyway, the idea of sporting illustrations had been a well-trodden road over the years — it would be much more effective if the illustrations were to arise 'naturally out of the text'. In other words, Charles Dickens offered a counterproposal in which he would write a novel in monthly instalments and Seymour would provide the illustrations. Then there was the name of the club: The Nimrod Club wasn't right; how about The Pickwick Club instead?

How Robert Seymour felt about his idea being taken over so comprehensively is unknown, for he committed suicide when only one of the monthly parts had been published.

The *Posthumous Papers of the Pickwick Club*, more commonly known as *The Pickwick Papers*, was published in monthly instalments from March '36 to October '37 and by its conclusion Boz's reputation as a bright new talent was firmly established.

Over the next years Dickens' reputation soared, with each successive novel being more popular than the previous one.

He didn't rely on simply re-hashing past successes either; for example, *Pickwick* had captured the public's imagination with its light comedy and farcical situations, whereas the next book, *Oliver Twist*, was dark, bleak and hard hitting, striking blow after blow against parochial hypocrisy and laying bare the lowest of London's lowlife.

Dickens now began to write constantly, producing book after book: *Nicholas Nickleby* ('38 – '39), *The Old Curiosity Shop* ('40 – '41), *Barnaby Rudge* ('41) and *Martin Chuzzlewit* ('42 – '44), and over the same period Catherine had given Charles four children.

The dynamic between the couple had changed now, for no longer was Charles an ambitious yet anonymous journalist; instead he was a celebrated author moving in circles peopled by the famous names in London literary society. He threw himself into every cause and accepted every invitation. Catherine often accompanied him to theatres and dinners and drew much praise for her wit and charm, but in the sparkling light of her effervescent husband she seemed, and felt, dull.

In 1842 the couple travelled to the United States of America, leaving their children in England, and spent four months travelling through the cities of Boston, New York and Washington DC as well as into the wilderness of the great plains. They were transported across the miles by steamboats, barges, coaches and, of course, railways. In his travelogue *American Notes* written after their return Dickens described the American rail system:

'I made acquaintance with an American railroad, on this occasion, for the first time. As these works are pretty much alike all through the States, their general characteristics are easily described.

'The cars are like shabby omnibuses, but larger: holding thirty, forty, fifty, people. The seats, instead of stretching from end to end, are placed crosswise. Each seat holds two persons. There is a long row of them on each side of the caravan, a narrow passage up the middle, and a door at both ends. In the centre of the carriage there is usually a stove, fed with charcoal or anthracite coal; which is for the most part red-hot. It is insufferably close; and you see the hot air fluttering between yourself and any other object you may happen to look at, like the ghost of smoke.

'The train calls at stations in the woods, where the wild impossibility of anybody having the smallest reason to get out, is only equalled by the apparently desperate hopelessness of there being anybody to get in. It rushes across the turnpike road, where there is no gate, no policeman, no signal: nothing but a rough wooden arch, on which is painted "When the Bell Rings, Look Out for the Locomotive"'.

'On it whirls headlong, dives through the woods again, emerges in the light, clatters over frail arches, rumbles upon the heavy ground, shoots beneath the wooden bridge which intercepts the light for a second like a wink, suddenly awakens all the slumbering echoes in the main street of a large town, and dashes on haphazard, pell-mell, neck-or-nothing, down the middle of the road.

'There, with mechanics working at their trades, and people leaning from their doors and windows, and boys flying kites and playing marbles, and men smoking, and women talking, and children crawling, and pigs burrowing, and unaccustomed horses plunging and rearing, close to the very rails, there, on, on, on, tears the mad dragon of an engine with its train of cars, scattering in all directions as shower of burning sparks from its wood fire, screeching, hissing, yelling, panting; until at last the thirsty monster stops beneath a covered way to drink, the people cluster round, and you have time to breathe again.'

The influence of the burgeoning railway system fascinated and terrified Dickens, for whilst he embraced progress and modernity he also hankered after a simpler, safer time. The newspapers were filled with lurid descriptions of terrible tragedies as society attempted to tame the raw power of the steam locomotive both by design and regulation.

The coming of the railways was a theme that Charles Dickens explored extensively in *Dombey and Son*, published between 1846 and 1848. In chapter 6 of the novel he described how Camden Town (his own childhood home, remember) was disfigured:

'The first shock of a great earthquake had, just at that period, rent the whole neighbourhood to its centre. Traces of its course were visible on every side. Houses were knocked down; streets broken through and stopped; deep pits and trenches dug in the ground; enormous heaps of earth and clay thrown up; buildings that were undermined and shaking, propped by great beams of wood. Here, a chaos of carts, overthrown and jumbled together, lay topsy-turvy at the bottom of a steep unnatural hill; there, confused treasures of iron soaked and rusted in something that had accidentally become a pond. Everywhere were bridges that led nowhere; thoroughfares that were wholly impassable; Babel towers of chimneys, wanting half their height; temporary wooden houses and enclosures, in the most unlikely situations; carcasses of ragged tenements, and fragments of unfinished walls and arches, and piles of scaffolding, and wildernesses of bricks, and giant forms of cranes, and tripods straddling above nothing. There were a hundred thousand shapes and substances of incompleteness, wildly mingled out of their places, upside down, burrowing in the earth, aspiring in the air, mouldering in the water, and unintelligible as any dream. Hot springs and fiery eruptions, the usual attendants upon earthquakes, lent their contributions of confusion to the scene. Boiling water hissed and heaved within dilapidated walls; whence, also, the glare and roar of flames came issuing forth; and mounds of ashes blocked up rights of way, and wholly changed the law and custom of the neighbourhood.

'In short, the yet unfinished and unopened Railroad was in progress; and, from the very core of all this dire disorder, trailed smoothly away, upon its mighty course of civilisation and improvement.'

Towards the end of the novel the villain of the piece, James Carker, gets his comeuppance on the line as he runs to escape:

'In the quick unsteadiness of the surprise, he staggered, and slipped on to the road below him. But recovering his feet immediately, he stepped back a pace or two upon that road, to interpose some wider space between them, and looked at his pursuer, breathing short and quick.

'He heard a shout — another — saw the face change from its vindictive passion to a faint sickness and terror — felt the earth tremble — knew in a moment that the rush was come — uttered a shriek — looked round — saw the red eyes, bleared and dim, in the daylight, close upon him — was beaten down, caught up, and whirled away upon a jagged mill, that spun him round and round, and struck him limb from limb, and licked his stream of life up with its fiery heat, and cast his mutilated fragments in the air.'

The latent danger of the great iron monsters that were ravaging the country was obvious to Charles Dickens twenty years before the events at Staplehurst.

Not only did Dickens fill his time by writing his novels; he also launched his own weekly journal *Household Words* which was first published in 1850. In January of that year Dickens wrote to his friend William Henry Wills offering him the post of sub-editor:

'My Dear Wills.

I have fully discussed the matter with Bradbury and Evans, on which we spoke today. We have concluded to make you the offer (which I hope may be satisfactory) of Eight Pounds a week absolutely, and one eighth share in all the profits of the Work, as well as of any other works that we may publish in connexion with it.

If you can let me know your decision on this proposal before we meet on Thursday, it may facilitate our business.

Faithfully Yours always CHARLES DICKENS'

Wills would be the man back at base, holding the fort, the man to look after the day to day running of the magazine whilst Charles travelled and wrote. He would remain in the post at *Household Words*, and later at its replacement *All The Year Round*, until Dickens' death in 1870 and would become one of his closest confidants and allies.

The magazine sold for tuppence and featured not only his own writing but also those of other authors, many younger, whose works Charles wished to champion. As well as fiction there were articles highlighting the plight of the working classes and underprivileged.

By the close of 1850 Catherine had given birth to five more children, bringing the total to nine, the youngest being a third daughter, Dora.

Throughout the early months of 1851 Dickens typically was working constantly, writing *David Copperfield* and ensuring that *Household Words* succeeded but in the middle of this whirlwind, towards the end of March, he received the terrible news that his father was seriously ill. Despite an emergency operation which he bore 'with astonishing fortitude, and I saw him directly afterwards — his room, a slaughter house of blood....' John would remain cheerful but grew ever weaker until he died peacefully on 31 March. Charles naturally was distraught but threw himself into arranging the funeral with his customary vigour.

No sooner had the formalities been completed and the ceremony at Highgate Cemetery been sorrowfully undertaken than more tragedy struck the Dickens family. Just two weeks later, on the 15th April, Charles wrote to Catherine who had been ill and was resting in the country:

'My dearest Kate.

Now observe. You must read this letter, very slowly and carefully. If you have hurried on thus far without quite understanding (apprehending some bad news), I rely on your turning back, and reading again.

Little Dora, without being in the least pain, is suddenly stricken ill. She awoke out of a sleep, and was seen, in one moment, to be very ill. Mind! I will not deceive you. I think her *very* ill.

There is nothing in her appearance but perfect rest. You would suppose her quietly asleep. But I am sure she is very ill, and I cannot encourage myself with much hope of her recovery. I do not — why should I say I do, to you my dear! — I do not think her recovery at all likely.

I do not like to leave home, I can do nothing here, but I think it right to stay here. You will not like to be away, I know, and I cannot reconcile it to myself to keep you away. Forster with his usual affection for us comes down to bring you this letter and to bring you home. But I cannot close it without putting the strongest entreaty and injunction upon you to come home with perfect composure — to remember what I have often told you, that we never can expect to be exempt, as to our many children, from the afflictions of other parents — and that if — *if* — when you come, I should even have to say to you "our little baby is dead", you are to do your duty to the rest, and to shew yourself worthy of the great trust you hold in them.

If you will only read this, steadily, I have a perfect confidence in your doing what is right. Ever affectionately

CHARLES DICKENS'

Although Charles had apparently been preparing Catherine for the worst by telling her that Dora was seriously ill and may possibly die soon, the truth of the matter was that she had already passed away during the previous evening, as Charles confessed to the philanthropist Angela Burdett-Coutts in another letter written two days later:

'My Dear Miss Coutts

Our poor little Dora! — I had just been playing with her, and went to preside at a Public Dinner to which I was pledged. Before it was over — even before they sang the Grace — she was dead. I had left her well and gay. My servant came down with the sad news, but they kept it from me until the meeting was over.

Mrs Dickens was at Malvern. By bringing her to town on a pretence of the poor little pet's being hopelessly ill, we made the shock as gradual as we could. She is as well as I could hope and begs me to say so to you and to thank you earnestly.

We laid the child in her grave today. And it is a part of the goodness and mercy of God that if we could call her back to life, now, with a wish, we would not do it.

Ever Most Faithfully Yours CHARLES DICKENS'

For the second time in a fortnight the Dickens family gathered tearfully in the little chapel at Highgate Cemetery.

From this time on Charles and Catherine became more distant, and Dickens began to find solace elsewhere in his longest and most enduring love: the theatre. He had always adored performing and as a young man in London he had taken a series of acting lessons with a view to making a career in the profession; he was never happier than when surrounded by theatrical folk and delighted in staging lavish amateur theatricals whenever he could.

During the dark months of 1851 he had used *Household Words* to launch The Guild of Literature and Arts which was an organisation created by Dickens and others to assist the families of artists who were left in poverty. The group, made up of notable names from the fields of literature, theatre and the visual arts would stage great theatrical events in order to raise money; of course, besides its philanthropic ideals, it was also a splendid excuse for Dickens to become an actor manager and indulge his passion for the stage.

Over the years the troupe performed plays such as Ben Johnson's *Every Man and his Humour*, and Elizabeth

Inchbald's farce *Animal Magnetism*, whilst Edward Bulwer-Lytton, another founder member of the Guild, wrote *Not So Bad As We Seem* which was performed in his ancestral home Knebworth House. What all these productions had in common was the name of Charles Dickens at the head of the cast list. He was supported by such luminaries as Wilkie Collins (now working with Charles at *Household Words*), the artist Augustus Egg and Mark Lemon, the editor of *Punch* magazine.

In 1856 Dickens suggested to Collins that they collaborate on a brand-new play which would be performed in Charles' own home in Tavistock Square and which was influenced by the doomed 1845 expedition undertaken by Sir John Franklin to find the North West Passage. The script, which was written by Wilkie, and called *The Frozen Deep*, avoided the scandal and rumour suggesting that the team had resorted to cannibalism in an effort to survive, but instead told a suitably melodramatic tale of love and self-sacrifice.

The date chosen for the performance was January 6th to mark the birthday of Charles's eldest son Charles junior, or Charley as he was known. Interest in London was great, and Charles Dickens began to convert his home into a theatre which would hold around 93 guests, at least ten of whom, as he wrote to Forster, 'will neither hear nor see!' His letters during the weeks prior to the performances described a flurry of preparation. He spoke of a great lighting effect that would open the show, 'I should very much like you only to see a Sunset — far better than anything that has ever been done at the Diorama or any such place. There is a Rehearsal to night (no one here but the company), and this Sunset, which begins the play, will be visible at a quarter before 8: lasting ten minutes.' Scenery had to be completed and he had enlisted two great artists to work on the backdrops. Clarkson Stanfield, a Royal Academician, was creating a splendid arctic vista for the final act, but Dickens wrote to him as if he were a stage hand at one of the London theatres, 'My Dear Stanny...I forgot that there are all those Icicles to be made. Could you manage to come tomorrow afternoon — direct that operation before dinner — take your mutton with us — and then take the Rehearsal? Do if you can.'

Catherine and the family were moved out of the house and the carpenters moved in.

There were to be four performances of the play and Dickens enlisted members of his own family to perform, including his daughters Mamie, who took on the difficult role of Clara, Katey and his sister-in-law Georgina Hogarth. The entire cast were rigorously rehearsed to a strict timetable until the day of the first performance arrived.

The *Illustrated London News* reported that Dickens' role of Richard Wardour 'required the consummate acting of a well-practised performer. Too much praise cannot be bestowed on the artistic interpretation that it received from him. It was a fervid, powerful and distinct individuality, thoroughly made out in all its details.' The same publication also journalistically patted Mamie, Katey and Georgina on the head as it praised their performances, 'The exceedingly natural manner in which these fair young creatures enacted and discoursed their sorrows gave to this private performance an advantage over any possible public representation; it was, in a word, exquisite.'

In the days after the performances, letters of congratulation, perhaps genuine, perhaps sycophantic, arrived and Charles, still aglow with the excitement, responded to them all:

'My Dear Lady Eastlake.

I must acknowledge the receipt of your kind note, because I have derived the greatest pleasure from it. No recognition of the *Art* of the representation, could be more valuable than yours and your good husband's; and you sum up in a single sentence all our aims and hopes as to the influences of that noble amusement which has unhappily been made so mean.

'…I hope our green curtain will not close for the last time next Wednesday night. Visions of another play in another year already rise before my mind's eye. If I write it myself, I shall desire no higher appreciation and sympathy to address it to, than yours and Sir Charles's — to whom I send my kind regard.

Always My Dear Lady Eastlake, Very faithfully Yours CHARLES DICKENS.'

The emptiness in Charles's life following his great success was palpable and he became restless to repeat the performance, missing the great camaraderie that went with the whole process of staging a play. His opportunity to re-form the company came on June 8th when his friend and fellow guild member Douglas Jerrold unexpectedly died. Dickens immediately decided that The Guild of Literature and Art should stage a special performance as a benefit for Jerrold's family, who actually asked him NOT to go ahead with the plan, fearing the humiliation that their perceived poverty would bring upon them, but Dickens was resolute and even had special stationery printed for the event; each letter sent in connection with the new endeavour was headed: 'IN REMEMBRANCE OF THE LATE MR DOUGLAS JERROLD. COMMITTEE'S OFFICE, GALLERY OF

ILLUSTRATION, REGENT STREET.'

In early July the performance took on a whole new level of importance. In an effort to build interest in the fundraising efforts Dickens had sent a letter to Colonel Phipps of the Royal household to see if Queen Victoria would lend her patronage to the Guild. Phipps replied saying that it would be impossible for the Queen to support such a cause because of the precedent it would set. However, she was keen to see the play and invited the entire troupe to Buckingham Palace for a private performance. Dickens refused to take the cast to the Palace, maybe because he did not wish his daughters to attend court in the guise of 'actresses', with all of the low associations that the word held at the time (this was the reason he gave to Angela Burdett-Coutts in a letter) or maybe because the preparations of the stage and special effects would be too lengthy and difficult, especially as they would need to be readied at Regent Street for the fundraising evening — he certainly would never countenance a sub-standard performance for such an audience, and the logistical problems would have been insurmountable.

Eventually it was agreed that there would be a private performance for the Queen at The Gallery of Illustration on July 4th with the main public presentation held on the following evening. To the delight of Dickens the Queen greatly enjoyed the play and was moved to send a note to the dressing rooms asking to meet so that she might congratulate him in person (in a letter to Forster Dickens suggested that the Monarch was 'begging me to go and see her and accept her thanks'), but in a fit of socialist pique Dickens refused, pointing out that he was in his farce costume and that it would not be appropriate to appear before her in anything but his own clothes. The Queen seemed to take the extraordinary snub in good grace, for she wrote to Dickens a few days later a letter which was of 'the most unofficial and uncourtly character'.

Once again, the general reaction to the play and in particular Charles's performance was overwhelming. One report with the headline 'Mr Charles Dickens As An Actor' wrote, 'Never was there a feeling of deeper and more genuine admiration than was left by Mr Charles Dickens in the minds of his auditors at the conclusion of Mr Wilkie Collins's drama *The Frozen Deep*. There was literally a gasp of applause when the curtain descended, and the conversation that ensued during the interval that preceded the farce was composed of laudatory criticism of details.'

The reporter went on to observe that 'the performance of Mr Dickens as the vindictive and (afterwards) penitent Richard Wardour is in the truest sense of the word a creation. Nay, we may go further and say that it is the creation of a literary man — that it is doubtful whether any mere actor, unless under the influence of some extraordinary sympathy with the part assumed, would attempt to fill up an outline with that elaborate detail that is introduced by Mr Dickens into Mr Collins' sketch.

'Where an ordinary artist would look for "points" of effect he looks for "points" of truth. A specimen of humanity in which every twitch of every muscle can be accounted for, is to be presented with all the elaboration of actual nature, no matter whether it be admired or not.'

The Morning Post added to that fulsome praise and went so far as to say that 'on the English stage there is no one who can approach him in his delineation of intense power and feeling.

'From first to last his performance was of the most finished nature, and that it was appreciated by the audience was evident from the constantly recurring hum of approbation, and frequent bursts of applause.'

The success of *The Frozen Deep*, and the publicity it had generated, convinced Charles that he should tour it more extensively. He had received an invitation to stage the play in Manchester and had initially declined citing the logistical difficulties of transporting the entire set and cast to the city, but the more he thought about it the more the idea appealed. The Free Trade Hall was chosen as the venue and Charles travelled north to view the space.

The Free Trade Hall, Manchester

Instantly he began to have doubts that his daughters would be able to cope with performing in such a cavernous venue and even as he travelled home, he wrote to Collins saying that, 'I have arranged to act *The Frozen Deep* in the Free Trade Hall on Friday and Saturday nights, the 21st and 22nd. It is an immense place, and we shall be obliged to have actresses... I am already trying to get the best who have been on the stage.' He also wrote to Francesco Berger, the composer and conductor who had created a score especially for the drama, reiterating his worries about the females, although, with the exception of his son Charley, he didn't seem to have any concerns as to whether any of the amateur males in the company could cope in such surroundings.

Dickens wrote to various actresses with whom he had acted in the past, but for various reasons they were unavailable, so he cast the net wider, asking his many contacts in the world of the theatre if they could suggest suitable candidates. Eventually Alfred Wigan, a playwright and actor, suggested a family of four ladies, mother and daughters, with whom he had worked. He trusted and admired them all and had no compunction in recommending them, and so it was that Charles Dickens first became aware of the Ternan family.

Charles and Ellen

Mrs Frances Ternan, or Fanny, had been born on the 8th February 1802, almost ten years to the day before Charles Dickens. She was the first child of John and Martha Jarman who themselves were theatrical folk working the Yorkshire theatres and in no time the baby was also appearing on stage. John died when Frances was only twelve years old, but her mother was a strong woman, for she gathered her two daughters together and created a family circle that would be recreated a generation later. Frances was a talented actress and soon was being noticed and talked of on the circuit, particularly in Ireland.

Without ever breaking into the very top level of theatre Frances continued to tour and in 1831 met and fell in love with an Irish actor named Thomas Ternan, who had spent much of his career playing the halls in Kent, particularly Rochester, the very city and theatres that Charles Dickens had explored as a child.

The couple married and toured extensively, including a successful spell in America, and during those years two daughters, Frances and Maria were born. In 1839 the Ternans returned to Kent, where Thomas's brother had settled, and it was in the great historic city of Rochester that Ellen Ternan was born, the same city to which the four members of The Pickwick Club, the first children of Charles Dickens' imagination, had travelled to begin their adventures three years before.

The Ternan family continued to travel, eking out as much of a living as they could manage. Maria and the younger Fanny were now taking larger roles and enjoying a degree of success and at the age of three Ellen joined them.

Unfortunately, Thomas Ternan's plans to become one of the great actor managers foundered and he slipped further into poverty and depression before dying in an insane asylum in 1846 leaving Frances to raise her three daughters in the same way that she herself had been raised. The theatrical community reached out to the distraught family, most particularly in the form of one of the great actor managers William Charles Macready, who would also become a great friend of Charles Dickens.

While Mrs Ternan, Fanny and Maria continued to earn a living, Ellen grew into her teenage years. The family moved to London where the older girls were working whilst 'the baby' stayed at home reading everything that she could get her hands on. Ellen loved to read and no doubt she devoured the latest offerings of Charles Dickens, who at this time was publishing *Little Dorrit*, the story of the little girl whose father is incarcerated in debtor's prison, having to make her way through the difficulties of a lonely life and eventually falling in love with an older, wealthy and apparently unobtainable man. No doubt she loved the romantic story and imagined herself in the dream of being desired and whisked away to greater things.

By the beginning of April 1857 Ellen, now 18, joined her sisters on the professional stage, and although she was possessed of no great talent, she engaged the raucous audiences of the day with her charm and innocence.

The professional Ternans were now a team of four: a family for hire.

When Charles Dickens approached Frances about booking her and her daughters to appear in *The Frozen Deep*, he was only able to secure three quarters of the troupe as the younger Frances was already committed to an engagement at The Princess's Theatre. Having met, and briefly rehearsed, the three actresses, arrangements were made for the company to travel to the North. The scene was like a circus leaving town as everyone gathered at Euston Station and boarded the train for Manchester. There was a sense of camaraderie, excitement and positivity within the party and the Ternans must have been somewhat starstruck in such exalted company. Ellen, the lover of literature, was surrounded by heroes who had glorified her childhood with their stories and the whole group was managed and bossed by Mr Charles Dickens himself! The great man seemed to be boisterous and loud as he led the gathering in games to pass the time and, no doubt, she was timid in his presence, scarcely daring to believe that the dream was actually real.

The journey north was a long one, but once the train arrived in Manchester the troupe made their way to The Great Western Hotel where Charles had reserved more than twenty lavish rooms, again something of an eye opener for the family of three who were more used to sharing squalid theatrical digs.

At the hall itself the preparations were in full flow with the stage being built by carpenters, the great painted backdrops that had been transported from London being hung, properties and furniture being placed and everywhere the loud shouts and ribald conversation that can be heard in any theatre in any city in any era. Adding to the general cacophony in the cavernous hall Signor Berger called the orchestra to attention and they began to rehearse.

The time for wide-eyed admiration was now passed for the Ternans as they had to rehearse their pieces and there was little time to spare: Mrs Ternan would be taking over the role of the old nurse from Georgina, whilst Maria would be taking over the important role of Clara from Mamie. Ellen had only a minor role in the main play and all three ladies also appeared in the farce *Uncle John* which concluded the evening.

The performances in Manchester were astounding and Dickens moved Maria to tears during his final speech of deathbed self-sacrifice (so effective was the speech that it would make a comeback in modified form in *A Tale of Two Cities* two years later). He described her face as 'a very good little pale face, with large black eyes — it had a natural emotion in it (although it was turned away from the audience) which was quite a study of emotion.

'At the same time, she sobbed, as if she were breaking her heart, and was quite convulsed with grief. It was no use for the compassionate Wardour to whisper, "My dear child, it will be over in two minutes — there is nothing the matter — don't be so distressed!" She could only sob out, "O! it's so sad, O it's so sad!" and set Mr Lemon (the softest hearted of men) crying too. By the time the curtain fell we were all crying together, and then her mother and sister used to come and put her in a chair and comfort her.'

Ellen was quietly in the background comforting her older sister, who seemed to be bewitching the great Charles Dickens.

The press heaped praise on the production as it had in London and the entire exercise was seen as a huge success. A considerable sum of money, over £2,000, had been raised for the Jerrold estate, but that seemed of secondary importance now.

At some stage during the run Charles Dickens had discovered that the Ternans, after finishing in Manchester, were due to travel to Doncaster where they had been engaged to play at the Theatre Royal. Excited by their vivacity, attracted by their talent and flattered by their attention, he quickly made plans to follow them.

Because of the efforts that he had expended on *The Frozen Deep* Charles had rather left *Household Words* to Wills, but had promised that after the show was done he would try to 'knock out a subject or two', and the prospect of a trip north, supposedly to collect material for a story, appealed to him. As soon as he was back in London he wrote to Wilkie Collins inviting (commanding) him to Gad's Hill Place to discuss ideas: 'Partly in the grim despair and restlessness of this subsidence from excitement, and partly for the sake of *Household Words*, I want to cast about whether you and I can go anywhere — take any tour — see anything — whereon we could write something together. Have you any idea, tending to any place in the world? Will you rattle your head and see if there is any pebble in it which we could wander away and play at Marbles with? We want something for *Household Words*, and I want to escape from myself. For, when I do start up and stare myself seedily in the face, as happens to be my case at present, my blankness is inconceivable — indescribable — my misery, amazing.'

It is amusing that Dickens asked Collins to suggest a location for their travels, for he knew exactly where they were going: Doncaster!

Dickens' melancholy and restlessness in the autumn of 1857 was borne of more than missing the bright lights of the stage, the camaraderie of the cast and the adulation of the audiences, for at this time his marriage to Catherine was collapsing hopelessly. He wrote candidly to John Forster that 'poor Catherine and I are not made for each other, and there is no help for it. It is not only that she makes me uneasy and unhappy, but that I make her so too — and much more so. She is exactly what you know, in the way of being amiable and complying; but we are strangely ill-assorted for the bond there is between us. God knows she would have been a thousand times happier if she had married another kind of man, and that her avoidance of this destiny would have been at least equally good for us both. I am often cut to the heart by thinking what a pity it is, for her own sake, that I ever fell in her way; and if I were sick or disabled to-morrow, I know how sorry she would be, and how deeply grieved myself, to think how we had lost each other. But exactly the same incompatibility would arise, the moment I was well again; and nothing on earth could make her understand me or suit us to each other. Her temperament will not go with mine. It mattered not so much when we had only ourselves to consider, but reasons have been growing since which make it all but hopeless that we should even try to struggle on. What is now befalling me I have seen steadily coming, ever since the days you remember when Mary was born; and I know too well that you cannot, and no one can, help me. Why I have even written I hardly know; but it is a miserable sort of comfort that you should be clearly aware how matters stand. The mere mention of the fact, without any complaint or blame of any sort, is a relief to my present state of spirits — and I can get this only from you, because I can speak of it to no one else.'

Whilst John Forster could be his confidant, Wilkie Collins could be his companion in rakish behaviour; the two authors' adventures would become known, for the sake of *Household Words*, as 'The Lazy Tour of Two Idle Apprentices' and would follow two literary gentlemen by the names of Mr Goodchild (Dickens) and Mr Idle (Collins) as they escaped from London. 'They had no intention of going anywhere in particular; they wanted to see nothing, they wanted to know nothing. They wanted to learn nothing, they wanted to do nothing. They wanted only to be idle.'

Once in Doncaster the two men booked tickets at The Theatre Royal where they watched the Ternans on stage and then introduced themselves afterwards. The following afternoon they attended the races and it is certain that they had the ladies for company throughout the day. Dickens, revelling in the vibrant company and feeling as if he was recapturing his own youth, bet on a few of the races and won a little money. The whole group delighted in the sheer joy of a late summer's excursion.

And from that day on Dickens pursued Ellen Ternan. She was 18 and he was 45.

As the relationship developed, with the consent and maybe even the encouragement of Mrs Ternan, so Dickens' life at home became more intolerable to him. He took to sleeping in a small dressing room and ordered that a partition wall should be built between it and the room where Catherine slept.

In May of 1858 he wrote to Angela Burdett-Coutts, with whom he had worked on numerous charitable causes since 1843, but who now firmly took Catherine's side, saying that 'I believe my marriage has been for years and years as miserable a one as ever was made. I believe that no two people were ever created, with such an impossibility of interest, sympathy, confidence, sentiment, tender union of any kind between them, as there is between my wife and me. It is an immense misfortune to her — it is an immense misfortune to me — but Nature has put an insurmountable barrier between us, which never in this world can be thrown down.' Warming to his theme he self-righteously continued, 'We have been virtually separated for a long time. We must put a wider space between us now, than can be found in one house.

'If the children loved her, or ever had loved her, this severance would have been a far easier thing than it is. But she has never attached one of them to herself, never played with them in their infancy, never attracted their confidence as they have grown older, never presented herself before them in the aspect of a mother. I have seen them fall off from her in a natural — not *un*natural — progress of estrangement, and at this moment I believe that Mary and Katey (whose dispositions are of the gentlest and most affectionate conceivable) harden into stone figures of girls when they can be got to go near her, and have their hearts shut up in her presence as if they closed by some horrid spring.

'No one can understand this, but Georgina who has seen it grow from year to year, and who is the best, the most unselfish, and the most devoted of human creatures.'

Rumours soon spread around London, initially suggesting that he was leaving his wife in favour of his sister-in-law Georgina Hogarth, who had lived with the couple since their marriage, and he fiercely denied them, publishing statements in the newspapers stating that 'I most solemnly declare, then

— and this I do, both in my own name and in my wife's name — that all the lately whispered rumours touching the trouble at which I have glanced, are abominably false. And that whoever repeats one of them after this denial, will lie as wilfully and as fouly as it is possible for any false witness to lie, before Heaven and Earth.' The target of his threats, among others, were the Hogarth family themselves which was now ripped apart with Catherine supported by her mother on one side, and her sister Georgina, aligning herself with Charles, on the other.

By 1858 Catherine had moved out of the family house at Tavistock Square and was living in a small house which Charles paid for, while Georgina, continuing to defy her own family, became his housekeeper, fiercely defending and protecting his reputation, and she would remain with him until the day of his death twelve years later.

1858 was a year of great change for Charles Dickens, for not only was there the domestic upheaval to contend with but he decided that the charitable readings that he had been giving over the past few years had proved so popular that it might be a good idea to develop them further so that he might derive an extra source of income, especially desirable now that he had two households and a mistress to support. Not only would there be a pecuniary benefit to him, but he had also the chance to travel, to be away from the rumour-mill in London, to be among his readers, his true friends.

Inevitably he threw himself completely into the new venture and performed 102 times between April and December of that year.

It was a strange dichotomy that whilst putting himself ever further into the public gaze he also desired to withdraw ever further from it. On 3rd September 1860 he gathered all his letters and papers from the past twenty years and cast them onto a huge bonfire in the grounds of Gad's Hill Place. His two youngest sons Henry and Edward (known in the family as 'Plorn') carried armfuls of papers to their apparently demonic father and watched him throw them into the flames. On the following day he described the scene to Wills, 'They sent up a smoke like the Genie when he got out of the casket on the seashore; and as it was an exquisite day when I began, and rained very heavily when I finished, I suspect my correspondence of having overcast the face of the Heavens.' The action was largely symbolic, for almost every letter that Charles Dickens had ever written was carefully kept by its recipient (naturally with the exception of the Ternan family) and would remain as a window into his life: Dickens sorrowfully observed that he wished he could have destroyed all of those letters too. He may have built the fire for many reasons but among them must surely have been a desire to hide his private life from ever increasing scrutiny.

The clandestine lives of Charles Dickens and Ellen Ternan continued over the next seven years, with him writing, travelling and performing, whilst keeping her existence and movements a closely guarded secret to all but his most intimate inner circle.

Until the summer of 1865.

PART TWO:
THE CRASH

Paris

On the morning of June 9th, 1865 Charles Dickens boarded the train in Paris accompanied by two ladies. One was Ellen Ternan and the other almost certainly her mother Fanny. Dickens had been in Paris for some time, and before leaving England had confided to John Forster that 'if I were not going away now, I should break down'. He had been complaining of ill health for some time and particularly of extreme pain in his left leg that he attributed to a 'neuralgic attack in the foot...' So swollen had it become that there were times that he couldn't even get his boot on. Today his condition would be described as gout.

But once in France he seemed to relax a little and wrote at the end of May that '...the moment I got away, I began, thank God, to get well'. The change of air and climate certainly seems to have had an efficacious effect on him, but maybe also there was the sense that a great decision had been reached, a weight lifted from his ageing shoulders, as he laid down plans for the future.

Charles Dickens loved Paris, as he did all lively exciting, bustling cities. He had first visited in 1844 as he travelled towards Italy, a trip which would provide the material and colour for his second travel book *Pictures From Italy*.

His arrival was on a Sunday morning and was delighted that the city was alive and welcoming rather than soberly observing the sabbath.

'There was, of course, very little in the aspect of Paris — as we rattled near the dismal Morgue and over the Pont Neuf — to reproach us for our Sunday travelling. The wine-shops (every second house) were driving a roaring trade; awnings were spreading, and chairs and tables arranging, outside the cafés, preparatory to the eating of ices, and drinking of cool liquids, later in the day; shoe-blacks were busy on the bridges; shops were open; carts and waggons clattered to and fro; the narrow, uphill, funnel-like streets across the river, were so many dense perspectives of crowd and bustle, parti-coloured nightcaps, tobacco-pipes, blouses, large boots, and shaggy heads of hair; nothing at that hour denoted a day of rest, unless it were the appearance, here and there, of a family pleasure-party, crammed into a bulky old lumbering cab; or of some contemplative holiday-maker in the freest and easiest dishabille, leaning out of a low garret window, watching the drying of his newly polished shoes on the little parapet outside (if a gentleman), or the airing of her stockings in the sun (if a lady), with calm anticipation.'

He would return often and would take the opportunity of being away from the attention and pressures of his London life, to write. There are plenty of letters from Paris describing his work, most alarmingly in 1846 as he worked on *Dombey and Son* the rather stark admission that 'Paul. I shall slaughter at the end of number 5'. In actuality the death of Little Paul Dombey is peaceful and serene and would become the focal point of one of his most popular public readings.

As in London, when not writing he would visit the theatres of Paris and in 1847 he reported that 'There is a melodrama, called *The French Revolution*, now playing at the

Cirque, in the first act of which there is the most tremendous representation of *a people* that can well be imagined. There are wonderful battles and so forth in the piece, but there is a power and massiveness in the mob which is positively awful.' He filed that storyline away in his mind and would return to it eleven years later.

Towards the end of 1862 he had a prolonged stay and rather than living in a hotel he rented an apartment on Rue du Faubourg, nestling in the triangle created by Boulevard Haussmann and the Avenue des Champs-Élysées which gave him wonderful access to all that Paris had to offer.

On 24th October of that year he wrote to his colleague at *All The Year Round* (his magazine had changed names from *Household Words* following a dispute with his publishers), William Henry Wills:

'We have a most elegant little apartment here; the lively street in front, and a splendid courtyard of great private hotels behind, between us and the Champs-Élysées. I have never seen anything in Paris, so pretty, airy, and light. But house rent is fearfully and wonderfully dear.

'High upon the Boulevard the old group of theatres that used to be so characteristic, is knocked to pieces, and preparations for some amazing new street are in rapid progress. I couldn't find my way yesterday to the Poste Restante, without looking at a map! — I suppose I have been there, at least 50 times before. Wherever I turn, I see some astounding new work, doing or done. When you come over here for the Xmas No. (as I think you must!) you shall see sights. Ever faithfully. CD'

Dickens returned to England on Christmas Eve of '62 and spent the festive season with his family at Gad's Hill Place, before returning to Paris early in the new year to perform two charity readings at the British Embassy.

'The state dinner at the Embassy, yesterday, coming off in the room where I am to read, the carpenters did not get in until this morning. But their platforms were ready — or supposed to be — and the preparations are in brisk progress. I think it will be a handsome affair to look at — a very handsome one. There seems to be great artistic curiosity in Paris, to know what kind of thing the reading is.' He wrote to his daughter Mary on January 16th.

As this trip was only supposed to be a short one, he did not take the apartment this time but stayed at the Hôtel du Helder, which was convenient for his reading on January 17th. As it happened the stay was much longer than he had planned, for the performance proved to be a remarkable success. Again, to Mary, he gushed: 'I cannot give you any idea of the success of the readings here, because no one can imagine the scene of last Friday night at the Embassy. Such audiences and such enthusiasm I have never seen, but the thing culminated on Friday night in a two hours' storm of excitement and pleasure. They actually recommenced and applauded right away into their carriages and down the street.

'You know your parent's horror of being lionised and will not be surprised to hear that I am half dead of it.'

To Wills he wrote that 'the French took to the Copperfield Reading, so astoundingly, that I am obliged to read twice more — on the 29th and 30th'.

Throughout his extended stay he remained in constant touch with Wills to ensure that *All The Year Round* was produced to his own exacting standards. He thoroughly enjoyed his stay at the Hôtel du Helder, declaring that '...I have dined better than I ever dined in Paris'.

The city would almost become a second home to Charles Dickens.

In *The Invisible Woman*, Claire Tomalin's definitive biography of Ellen Ternan, she points out that during the period prior to June 1865 it is impossible to know what had been happening with Ellen, as there is absolutely no record of her whereabouts or movements.

The fact that Ellen did not attend her sister's wedding in England, and more surprisingly neither did her mother, suggests that they were together and that there were pressing reasons to remain together in seclusion. Charles Dickens had made many more trips than usual to Paris during the same period and it seems most likely that Ellen and Frances were living in the city or nearby. It is now thought almost inevitable that there was a baby boy born during this period. In her 1939 book *Dickens and Daughter* Gladys Storey asserted that Charles and Ellen had a son. Her sources for this information appear to be two of Dickens' children Katey and Henry who confided in her separately. Henry spoke to her in 1928 and intimated 'that there was a boy, but it died'.

Claire Tomalin brilliantly sums up the situation by pointing out that 'there is no hard evidence that Nelly had a child; but there is too much soft evidence to be brushed aside entirely'.

Taking Katey's and Henry's words as the truth, and neither of them had anything to gain by inventing such a story, it would appear that the son died in infancy, possibly in childbirth, and this is the reason that Ellen needed her mother with her, to care and comfort. These months in Paris, if indeed that is where they were, must have affected the relationship between Ellen and Charles and the loss of their son brought that lively and exciting period of their life together to a tragic and sorrowful end.

Things could never be the same again. Charles had already experienced the same grief and confusion when he and Catherine had lost Dora thirteen years earlier.

There are no letters from Dickens in the early days of June but it may be supposed that he was staying back at The Hôtel du Helder on the night of June 8th, for the travellers needed to rise early and take a carriage to the station, and the hotel, well known to him, was convenient for that purpose.

At 7 o'clock the next morning the little group arrived at the Gare du Nord ready to board their train. Dickens in his greatcoat and top hat, the ladies wrapped in their shawls and bonnets.

The great terminus had only been opened the year before and indeed was not yet complete, but it was a magnificent edifice and one which celebrated the new and exciting world of trans-continental rail travel.

Paris, Gare du Nord, 1865

The luggage was loaded, and Ellen carried a large collection of gold jewellery with her, which suggests that the trio were planning a permanent return home, for it is unlikely that she would bring so many valuable items for a short visit to England.

It was not only Ellen who travelled with a valuable cargo, for within the voluminous pockets of his coat Charles had the handwritten manuscript of part 16 of his current novel *Our Mutual Friend*. As soon as he arrived in London, he planned to take a hansom cab to the offices of *All The Year Round* in Wellington Street and hand the papers directly to Wills so that they could be prepared for publication.

So important was the document to Dickens that he didn't even put it into the large Gladstone bag that he typically travelled with, for that could easily have been mislaid, forgotten or stolen; much better to keep it close to him at all times. In just a few hours his fears about being separated from the bag would be violently realised.

As Paris awoke, as the engineer pulled the cord to sound the train whistle and released the brake, as the passengers settled into their seats, they felt the first jolt of motion that began a ten-hour journey to London. Over two hundred miles away in the middle of a marshy field the first, apparently inconsequential, acts of a tragedy were being played out.

Staplehurst

The county of Kent, which nestles in the south-eastern peninsular of the British Isles, is known as 'the Garden of England' and traditionally is an agricultural region, especially well known for producing fine fruits. Charles Dickens himself summed up the county in *The Pickwick Papers* when the itinerant actor Mr Jingle pronounced, 'Kent, sir — everyone knows Kent — apples, cherries, hops and women.'

Whilst numerous orchards supplied the apples and cherries, it was the hop fields that gave the Kentish landscape its unique appearance. Hops were, and are, used in the production of beer to help stabilise the English ale as well as giving it the distinctive bitter flavour for which it is renowned.

Hop plants, which are part of the hemp family, are grown up strings attached to huge frames, and the stringing is done in the winter months before there is any growth. Throughout the spring the plants, which are perennial, break the surface and by June are growing up the strings. In July and August, the fruit forms, and by September they are ready to be harvested. Today, of course, the harvest is mechanised, but in the 19th century, when the hop industry in Kent was at its height, a huge workforce was needed to complete the job before the harsh rains of the autumn and winter ruined the season's crop.

Hop Picking, c. 1900s

Whole families would travel from London into Kent where they lived in tiny shacks on the hop farms to work the fields. Not only were the wages an essential part of many families' survival but the trips also served as a great communal holiday away from the squalor and danger of the city. Rivalries would spring up between the Kentish locals and the incomers, sometimes villagers boarding up their shops when the 'invasion' took place. There was not only distrust, however, and often strong friendships, even romances, were forged. It is extraordinary that Dickens didn't write about the hop pickers, for he witnessed their suffering at first hand. In a letter to John Forster from Gad's Hill Place he wrote, 'Hop-picking is going on, and people sleep in the garden, and breathe in at the keyhole of the house door. I have been amazed, before this year, by the number of miserable lean wretches, hardly able to crawl, who go hop-picking. I find it is a superstition that the dust of the newly picked hop, falling freshly into the throat, is a cure for consumption. So the poor creatures drag themselves along the roads, and sleep under wet hedges, and get cured soon and finally.' It sounds like perfect material for a Dickensian plot set among the twines and frames of the Kentish hop fields.

Between the North and South Downs (two gentle ridges of hills stretching across the countryside from east to west) nestles a lowland area known as the Weald of Kent and it is in this huge valley that some of the most productive hop fields were situated. Even today if you drive south from the county town of Maidstone, you will find plenty of the distinctive oast houses scattered throughout the countryside.

Originally built to dry the hops, oast houses were constructed with a conical roof, complete with a white cowl at the top. Kilns were lit at the base of the oast and the hops were laid out on slatted trays above the embers. The cowl at the apex of the roof could swing around with the wind, allowing the smoke to be drawn up through the drying trays and away.

These days most oast houses have been converted into extremely desirable and expensive homes, but their presence in the Kentish landscape is a reminder of their economic importance to the region.

The oldest oast house still in existence, dating back to 1740, is situated in the Wealden town of Sissinghurst, which is just four miles from the ancient Anglo-Saxon village of Staplehurst.

The main river in Kent is the Medway, which roughly cuts the county in half before joining the mighty Thames as they both feed into the North Sea at Sheerness. Tradition has it that if a man is born to the west of the Medway he is known as a

Kentish Man, whereas those born to the east are Men of Kent. As it makes its way to the sea the Medway is fed by numerous tributaries such as the Tease, the Loose, the Eden, the Bourne and the River Beult which rises near Woodchurch and meanders prettily and inconsequentially through the countryside before joining the Medway to the north of Paddock Wood. It is not a large river but the villages along its route are perfect examples of ancient Kentish architecture and at one point it is spanned by 'Town Bridge', the longest Medieval bridge in the country.

To the east of Staplehurst the Beult twists and turns this way and that so that a ramrod-straight stretch of railway track crosses it on three different occasions within a very short distance.

Each crossing point necessitated a small viaduct and in 1865 the three bridges were built of brick carrying lengths of iron and timber which supported the rails, allowing the daily trains to travel swiftly to and from London.

In the spring and summer of 1865, over a period of almost ten weeks, each of the bridges had been undergoing repair, for the timbers had become damp and rotten. The team who worked on this project was made up of four carpenters, four platelayers and one labourer, all being under the leadership of Henry Benge. Benge's official title was 'The Foreman of The Platelayers', which sounded impressive and gave the impression of a strong leader of men with a background in engineering, but Henry's entry in the 1861 UK census listed him simply as an 'Agricultural Labourer'. He had been appointed to his post a few years earlier by Joseph Gallimore who held the position of the Inspector of Permanent Way, which gave him overall responsibility for the safety of the line in that particular part of Kent. Benge had been given a book containing a set of rules which he was required to read, and for his extra duties he was paid a guinea each week, as opposed to the 18 shillings paid to the regular labourers.

The work on the three viaducts crossing the Beult involved lifting a stretch of rail and laying it at the side of the way whilst the rotten timber was removed and replaced. When the new structure was secured safely into the iron girders the rails could be replaced and the keys which held it firmly in place tightened. Each section of track could be removed and replaced in about 75 minutes and therefore could be completed during the times when no trains were running on the line.

The crew's routine had become settled over the weeks, to that extent that a degree of laziness had crept into their labours. The work had been commissioned by Gallimore, and because the job did not involve an extended closure of the line it was not regarded as a 'protracted repair'. If it had been thus categorised, Gallimore would have been required to make regular visits to the site and report to Mr Ashcroft, the chief engineer of the South Eastern Railway. Astoundingly, in June 1865 Ashcroft was not even aware that there were any works taking place near Staplehurst.

A job lasting ten weeks should certainly have been listed as a protracted repair, but Gallimore's decision meant that each day was seen as a separate operation and so it was that one failsafe was overlooked.

On the morning of June 9th, 1865 Henry Benge and his team began work at 6.00 am and after two hours of work they broke to take their breakfast. As they ate, the foreman took out his timetable book to check what time the tidal train from Folkestone was due.

At the same time in a siding at Folkestone Junction station George Crombie, a train driver with eleven years' experience with the South Eastern Railway Company, was beginning the long process of preparing locomotive 199 for its day's work. The small fire that had burned through the night keeping the boiler warm was heaped with Welsh coal, building into the roaring inferno that would power the locomotive throughout the day. Having stoked the furnace Crombie methodically made his way around the engine, oiling and greasing every moving part.

Boulogne

Eduard Manet: The Folkestone Boat, Boulogne

In France Dickens and the Ternans settled themselves into their first-class carriage as the train pulled out of the Gare du Nord and rhythmically made its way towards Amiens, through Abbeville and towards the quayside in Boulogne.

What was the atmosphere like in the carriage? Who can tell? One may suppose that Ellen herself would have been reflective, distant, uneasy, whilst Dickens, the great wordsmith, felt awkward, finding the circumstance beyond his experience. His wife Catherine had suffered a number of miscarriages over the years, as well as the loss of Dora, but this was different, and he was ill prepared for such emotional turmoil. For one who wove words so eloquently his inability to comfort Ellen, to find the right vocabulary, was confusing, and all his attempts at conversation were stilted and inane. In response to his clumsy efforts Ellen snapped at him curtly and returned to her own innermost thoughts.

Surely Mrs Ternan made efforts to lighten the mood, to act as mediator and to try and reconcile the lovers?

The journey to Boulogne occupied almost four hours and the three passengers eventually subsided into silence and gazed through the window, not really seeing the landscape as it flashed by, not taking in the beautiful sun in a cloudless sky or the fields burgeoning with their crops. Perhaps Dickens took the manuscript of *Our Mutual Friend* from his pocket to study and read over it once more, mentally correcting a certain passage and losing himself in his fictional world where he felt safe.

Eventually the familiar buildings of Boulogne, dominated by the great but as yet unfinished Basilica of Notre Dame sitting proudly in the ramparts of the old walled town, came into sight and the passengers on board the train began to make preparations for leaving the little cocoons of their compartments. Charles knew Boulogne particularly well, for the family had spent a few summers there in happier times and he wrote glowingly about it in *Our French Watering Place*, published in 1854.

His first observations reflected the journey he now made from Paris:

'...once solely known to us as a town with a very long street, beginning with an abattoir and ending with a steam-boat, which it seemed our fate to behold only at daybreak on winter mornings, when (in the days before continental railroads), just sufficiently awake to know that we were most uncomfortably asleep, it was our destiny always to clatter through it, in the coupe of the diligence from Paris, with a sea of mud behind us, and a sea of tumbling waves before.'

The settlement now known as Boulogne sits at the mouth of the Liane River and was first settled by the Romans, although no doubt there was previously a fishing port nestling in the natural harbour before that. The Roman settlement was originally known as Gesoriacum before the name was changed to Bononia.

With Claudius's invasion of Britain in AD 45 Boulogne became an important staging post and the great Classis Britannica fleet was moored in the harbour before setting out across the channel for the Roman port of Richborough near Sandwich from where the might of the Roman army, as well as such supplies that the new outposts of the empire required, were dispatched. The way north was called Watling Street and it began at a huge triumphal arch which dominated the Kentish landscape before making its way towards Canterbury and Rochester. The ancient route would remain in use long after the Romans had retreated to warmer climes and it became the main thoroughfare from London to the south coast. Near to the town of Gravesend it passed the small village of Higham and the house at the top of Gad's Hill that would later become the home of Charles Dickens.

As with any strategic coastal town sieges and battles to secure Boulogne were numerous. It was destroyed by the Normans in 882 before being rebuilt in 912. At around this time the Greek scholar Zosimus referred to it as Germanorum which translated means 'German speaking', giving an idea as to its desirability to all nationalities and empires.

In the 11th century the city stood proudly on the shore and one of its most influential counts Eustace II became a trusted ally of William of Normandy as he planned his invasion of Britain. Eustace fought gallantly at Senlac Hill (near to Hastings and now known as the town of Battle), playing an important part in defeating the defending Saxons led by King Harold. In honour of his service Eustace was awarded great tracts of English land by William and it is thought that he might have been responsible for commissioning the Bayeux Tapestry.

With its natural resources (it was a major centre for whale and herring fishing), as well as its strategic position at the mouth of the Liane Boulogne was fought over constantly throughout the course of the 100 Years War, and ownership changed from French to English and back again many times. Even after the Peace treaty of Étaples was agreed, bringing the conflict to a close and returning Calais and Boulogne to the French King, the two nations continued to squabble, and Boulogne was once again taken by the English in 1544. It was not until 1550 that the city was purchased for 400,000 crowns and settled into its French identity permanently.

In the early 1800s the Emperor Napoleon followed the example set by Claudius almost 1,800 years before by planning to use the city as base from which to launch his invasion of Britain. The Flotilla de Boulogne was built and mustered, as the Classis Britannica had been before, and the soldiers lay in wait for the word from their leader. Napoleon himself visited the troops often and in a great show of pomp staged a ceremony on the beach at which he awarded the very first légions d'honneur.

A huge column was erected on the clifftop ready to celebrate Napoleon's success, but the invasion plans were those of an army man, not a naval one, and the British fleet easily overpowered the French, scoring great victories at Finisterre and Trafalgar. The invasion eventually was called off, but today the column still stands with the figure of Napoleon atop it firmly facing AWAY from the English coast.

With the coming of the railways Boulogne became a popular and fashionable venue for Parisian tourists, and the cross-channel steamers brought the wealthy and respectable folk from England. Indeed, there grew quite an English colony in the city. Mr Merridew Mellville, originally from Coventry, was one of the incomers and in 1844 he was granted permission to open a bookshop in the town and later he formed The British and Foreign Library which was based, appropriately, on Rue Victor Hugo.

In 1853 Charles Dickens settled in Boulogne for the first time, staying at the Villa des Mollineux for a month, and it would appear as if he were auditioning the town to replace Broadstairs as the family's summer base. Boulogne obviously passed that audition, for the following year he returned with the entire family and set up camp in the Villa du Camp de droit for three months, 'I think the finest situation (Genoa excepted) I ever lived in, and the best cottage house. It beats the former residence all to nothing.'

Charles liked to spend long summers with his family, and although he would occasionally travel back to London, or invite friends and colleagues to join the party for extended periods of time, these holidays were essentially a necessary break from the grind of his everyday city existence.

The summers by the sea endeared Boulogne to the Dickens family and the images he recorded in *Our French Watering Place* are infectious, indeed: long days bathing, attending the opera and becoming inseparable from their

French hosts. Who can resist the '…well-paved main streets, towards five o'clock in the afternoon, when delicate odours of cookery fill the air, and its hotel windows (it is full of hotels) give glimpses of long tables set out for dinner, and made to look sumptuous by the aid of napkins folded fan-wise, you would rightly judge it to be an uncommonly good town to eat and drink in'?

Not only did he explore the main avenues and the bustling marketplace, but also the extraordinary neighbourhood called The Beurières, which was spread across five streets each so steep that they were paved with stone steps and not cobbles. On either side of each street three-storied houses were crammed together and each floor of each house was the home for one family — up to eleven people living in two small rooms, and it was recorded during the 19th century that 13,000 people lived within the five streets. Children slept on rudimentary cots built into kitchen cupboards to save space, whilst the babies were put down to sleep and shut away in chests of drawers. There was no running water to these houses, no drainage, no sanitation and the effluent would be disgorged into the street, cascading down the steps in a foul-smelling waterfall. All the tenants were fishing folks and their homes were rented from the owners of the boats who lived in much grander accommodations on the quayside. Rivalries and fights were commonplace, but these were people united in their profession and when a man was lost at sea (as often happened), the community came together to help the grieving family. It was just the sort of neighbourhood that Dickens loved to explore and write about in the nature of Tom-All-Alones in *Bleak House* (although the latter was a hopeless slum whereas The Beurières were a hive of industry).

Henry Fielding Dickens, just four years old when the

family first stayed in the city, had vague memories of their temporary house and wrote of 'lovely gardens straggling up the hillside with a blaze of bright colours, and a picturesque kind of chalet called "Tom Pouce" which was reserved for Wilkie Collins when he was staying there'. Today an expensive condominium with fine views across the sea sits on the site of the old house and the narrow street that leads to the gate is the Rue Charles Dickens.

So much did Charles Dickens admire the fishing port that he sent three of his sons Alfred, Sidney and Henry to be educated at Miss Gibson's Boarding School situated in the town. A knowledge of the French language was a necessity in Charles's mind and he himself spoke the language fluently (many of his letters from France are written in French). Such was the impression left upon young Henry that he would go on to marry a French woman himself, Marie Roche, and proposed to her on the old ramparts.

Considering the happiness which the Dickens family had enjoyed in Boulogne it is perhaps surprising that Charles should bring Ellen Ternan back to the region after the rancorous separation from Catherine, but with an extraordinary lack of sentimentality or sensitivity, the couple enjoyed long stays together in their 'Love Nest' at Condette, little more than six miles away from the beaches where the children had laughed and frolicked just a few years before.

At around midday on June 9th the train arrived at La Gare Maritime and the passengers disembarked, ready to face the next part of their journey. As Dickens helped Ellen and Frances from the compartment so the porters were already unloading the trunks and cases and loading them onto carts to transfer them to the steam packet that bobbed and rocked gently in readiness for its voyage.

There was a short walk to the ship, across a bridge, past the bustling fish market which gave, and still gives, Boulogne its distinctive smell, along the Quai Gambetta, past the fleet of fishing boats towards the elegant casino which overlooked a stretch of beach where bathing huts were pulled to and from the gentle surf by donkeys. The passengers made their way with different degrees of rapidity, some on foot, some in hansom cabs, to the spot towards the end of the quay where the luggage was already piled high waiting to be stowed. It was midday and the bells of Notre Dame and St Pierre provided the city's never-changing soundtrack with their doleful and monotonous tolling,

How was Dickens perceived at this time? In Paris it is possible that he and his companions were unnoticed in the bustle of the great station, but now among a small huddle of fellow passengers there could be no hiding. On one such trip he was seen by a disapproving Clare Byrne, whose husband owned the *Morning Post* newspaper. According to her account it seems that Charles made no effort to shrink from the public eye or even to conceal his companion:

'Travelling with him was a lady not his wife, nor his sister-in-law, yet he strutted about the dock with the air of a man bristling with self-importance, every line of his face and every gesture of his limbs seemed haughtily to say — "look at me; make the most of your chance. I am the great, the *only* Charles Dickens."'

The 9th of June was a warm day and the small group stood on the quayside discussing the issues of the day. Perhaps some even conjectured on the continuing plot of *Our Mutual Friend*, little knowing that the answer lay in a pocket just a matter of feet away. The ladies, who had earlier been wrapped in their shawls against the chill of a Paris morning, now protected themselves from the bright sun beneath delicate parasols.

As they chatted Charles Dickens was greeted by Mr Melville, the proprietor of the Library, who would be joining the passengers and journeying to England. Of course, Charles had spent a great deal of time in Mr Melville's establishment and welcomed his good friend and compatriot.

Among the group was Amelia Rayner travelling home to Liverpool where her husband Lloyd, a successful and respected merchant, would be waiting for her. It had been a month since they had last seen one another, and she was keen to return home to her family. She travelled with her eleven-year-old son Lloyd junior and her sister-in-law.

Annie Bodenham stood hand in hand with her husband Frederick, for even though the couple had married more than two years earlier in Devon, they were just now returning from their wedding tour of Europe. Frederick was a partner in his family's firm of solicitors James and Bodenham in Hereford. Charlotte Faithful, an elegant and worldly woman, was travelling back to London where she would be reunited with her husband who was a judge in India. Charlotte herself had been travelling in the East and most recently had been staying in Egypt.

Monsieur Marchant, an officer in the French Navy, would board the steamer and return to his natural element. Although the calm seas of the day would probably have disappointed him, he would take a position at the bow like a great carved figurehead.

Adam Hampson and his wife Elizabeth had been staying at The Castle and Falcon hotel in London a few days earlier but had heard of a special train excursion to Paris and decided to join the tour. Adam was a respected surgeon in Bolton.

These and many more mingled on the dock waiting to board the steamer.

It was a scene that was repeated every day and one which was captured a few years later by Eduard Manet in his painting *The Folkestone Boat, Boulogne*.

It is likely that the Dickens party would have been sailing on either the *Victoria* or the *Albert Edward* steamers, for they were the newest, largest and fastest vessels in the South Eastern Railway's fleet. They weighed in at 374 tons and had been built in 1861 and 1862, respectively, by Samuda Brothers at their yard on the Isle of Dogs in London.

The sister ships were propelled through the water by two huge paddle wheels, covered with gleaming white shrouds and the smoke was taken from the boilers through twin raked funnels which gave a wonderful impression of speed, as did the elegant clipper bow and long bowsprits which reached out to a far horizon.

At 12:15 the ropes were released, the steamer slipped her moorings and slowly made her way to the harbour mouth, protected by two long walls stretching like clutching skeletal fingers into La Manche. Once clear of the harbour the captain increased the speed of the paddles and made a heading for Folkestone.

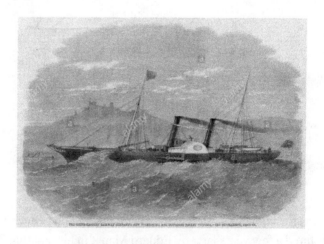

Staplehurst

The scene at the site of the final viaduct before Staplehurst station was one of hard work and intense industry at midday on the 9th June, 1865. For over ten weeks the team had been replacing the old, rotting timber baulks on which the metal rails lay from the other two bridges which crossed the Beult, and were now working on the final stretch. Of the thirty-two baulks that needing replacing, twenty-nine had been completed. The end was in sight.

The work had continued safely, even though the inspector of the permanent way had not supervised the process as he should have done, and there was no reason to suppose that anything was particularly amiss on that morning. At 2:50 a local train was due on the up line, so the timbers and rails were replaced to allow it through safely, and at 2:51 the work resumed and the timbers were removed once more.

Earlier that day it had been the job of the foreman, Henry Benge, to study the complicated timetable booklet to ascertain exactly what time the tidal train would thunder through (due to the vagaries of the tide in the Channel the service did not leave Folkestone at a regular time). Benge was seen by his team studying the book at breakfast. The local train was due at 2:50 and Henry told the crew that the tidal train, the express, was not expected until 5:20 pm, giving them plenty of time to complete the day's work. Unfortunately, his cursory look at the pages had been insufficient to take in the correct facts. He was actually reading the page for the 10th June, instead of the 9th and the train was in fact due at 3:15 pm: two full hours earlier.

To ensure that such a basic error could not have been committed safety protocol demanded that there be a second timetable book held by the head carpenter, John Dawson, and that both should have been studied together. Unfortunately, the carpenter's book had been cut in two by a locomotive wheel running over it and hadn't been replaced. There was no worry among the crew, however, for Benge had led them well and there had been no issue during the preceding weeks. As well as the local train, one single locomotive and two ballast trains had used the tracks that day but were signalled to stop, which they successfully did before reaching the breach in the line. Otherwise the baulks and rails had all been daily replaced before the passenger trains arrived.

The lack of the second timetable book was another failsafe that had been ignored.

Of course, signalling was a vital issue to maintain the safety not only of the passengers, but also of the working party themselves, so one member of the team was given the job of stationing himself along the line with a red danger flag to display. The labourer, John Wiles, was to position himself 1,000 yards away from the work, which distance would give a locomotive travelling at full steam plenty of room to shut off and stop safely, as had been the case on the three previous occasions.

Despite the hitherto exemplary safety record there were so many oversights on the 9th June that disaster was almost inevitable. Not only had Mr Benge read the timetable incorrectly, and there was no second copy to consult, but that error was compounded by the fact that Wiles decided to judge the 1,000 yards distance by counting telegraph poles, which he guessed to be about 100 yards apart. He was wrong, for having walked beyond a spot where a cattle track crossed the rails, called Sloman's Crossing, he settled himself just 554 yards from the viaduct — only half the distance required.

Regulations also demanded that the signalman be issued with five explosive charges, or fog signals, two of which were to be placed ten yards apart at the point where the red flag was displayed, and then at distances of 250 yards leading up to the breach. These charges would detonate as a train passed, thereby sending an audible warning to the driver and guards that there was danger ahead. Wiles was given only two charges and instructed not to use them unless foggy conditions prevailed, but the day was bright and sunny, so he didn't place them.

Two more failsafes had been ignored.

The local train arrived on time and the team had carefully replaced the timbers and the rails to allow it safe passage. As soon as it was past, they began to dismantle the bridge once more in the belief that they had over two hours to complete the final section of their work.

The rest of the workers started to replace the three remaining baulks, confident in the knowledge that they had plenty of time to work, 554 yards away from where John Wiles sat.

At Headcorn station, a mile back along the line, the signals remained in the 'all clear' position.

At Sea

The Steamships *Victoria* and *Albert Edward* both had a top speed of 12 ½ knots and would have made the crossing from Boulogne to Folkestone in around two and a half hours. The deck space was mainly open (although the *Victoria* would later have a cover over the fore deck), which not only left the passengers exposed to the elements and the spray, but also meant that anyone wanting some privacy would be disappointed. Charles Dickens wasn't a great sailor and probably sat huddled tightly, wrapped up in his great coat, despite the sunny day, waiting for the voyage to end.

It was a voyage that Dickens was very familiar with and in *Our French Watering Place* he described his arrival at port (in that case Boulogne):

'In the first place, the steamer no sooner touches the port, than all the passengers fall into captivity: being boarded by an overpowering force of Custom-house officers, and marched into a gloomy dungeon. In the second place, the road to this dungeon is fenced off with ropes breast-high, and outside those ropes all the English in the place who have lately been sea-sick and are now well, assemble in their best clothes to enjoy the degradation of their dilapidated fellow-creatures. "Oh, my gracious! How ill this one has been!" "Here's a damp one coming next!" "HERE'S a pale one!" "Oh! Ain't he green in the face, this next one!"'

The truth is that Charles Dickens was not comfortable at sea.

In 1842 Dickens, at that time a young, brash, opinionated and arrogant young man had set sail from Liverpool to America and endured one of the worst storms that the North Atlantic had seen for many years. Shortly after his arrival he wrote of his discomfort to his friend Thomas Mitton:

'We had a dreadful passage, the worst, the officers all concur in saying, that they have ever known. We were eighteen days coming; experienced a dreadful storm which swept away our paddle-boxes and stove our lifeboats; and ran aground besides, near Halifax, among rocks and breakers, where we lay at anchor all night. After we left the English Channel, we had only one fine day.'

In his memoir of the trip *American Notes for General Circulation* Charles described the crossing with his customary theatrical and journalistic zeal:

'It is the third morning. I am awakened out of my sleep by a dismal shriek from my wife, who demands to know whether there's any danger. I rouse myself and look out of bed. The water-jug is plunging and leaping like a lively dolphin; all the smaller articles are afloat, except my shoes, which are stranded on a carpet-bag, high and dry, like a couple of coal-barges. Suddenly I see them spring into the air, and behold the looking-glass, which is nailed to the wall, sticking fast upon the ceiling. At the same time the door entirely disappears, and a new one is opened in the floor. Then I begin to comprehend that the state-room is standing on its head.

'Before it is possible to make any arrangement at all compatible with this novel state of things, the ship rights. Before one can say "Thank Heaven!" she wrongs again.

Before one can cry she IS wrong, she seems to have started forward, and to be a creature actually running of its own accord, with broken knees and failing legs, through every variety of hole and pitfall, and stumbling constantly. Before one can so much as wonder, she takes a high leap into the air. Before she has well done that, she takes a deep dive into the water. Before she has gained the surface, she throws a summerset. The instant she is on her legs, she rushes backward. And so she goes on staggering, heaving, wrestling, leaping, diving, jumping, pitching, throbbing, rolling, and rocking: and going through all these movements, sometimes by turns, and sometimes altogether: until one feels disposed to roar for mercy.

'A steward passes. "Steward!" "Sir?" "What IS the matter? What DO you call this?" "Rather a heavy sea on, sir, and a head-wind."

'A head-wind! Imagine a human face upon the vessel's prow, with fifteen thousand Samsons in one bent upon driving her back and hitting her exactly between the eyes whenever she attempts to advance an inch. Imagine the ship herself, with every pulse and artery of her huge body swollen and bursting under this maltreatment, sworn to go on or die. Imagine the wind howling, the sea roaring, the rain beating: all in furious array against her. Picture the sky both dark and wild, and the clouds, in fearful sympathy with the waves, making another ocean in the air. Add to all this, the clattering on deck and down below; the tread of hurried feet; the loud hoarse shouts of seamen; the gurgling in and out of water through the scuppers; with, every now and then, the striking of a heavy sea upon the planks above, with the deep, dead, heavy sound of thunder heard within a vault; — and there is the head-wind of that

January morning.'

So grateful had Charles and his fellow passengers been on that occasion that they collected £50 and purchased an inscribed plate for the captain of the ship, Captain Hewitt:

'As a slight acknowledgment of his great ability and skill under circumstances of much difficulty and danger, and as a feeble token of their lasting gratitude.'

From 1853 Charles crossed the English Channel frequently, for his visits to both Paris and Boulogne, and it seems that he was never possessed of sturdy sea legs, which is perhaps surprising considering his happiest childhood days had been spent exploring the Royal Dockyards at Chatham and mixing with the sailors as they returned from exotic climes. Many of his descendants would go on to have careers at sea but their abilities and desire to span the oceans were apparently not inherited from Charles Dickens himself.

Folkestone

At around 2 pm the steamer of the South Eastern Railway neared Folkestone Harbour and prepared to dock at the new pier which had been built into the Channel from the old quay in 1863 to allow the new larger ships to dock safely without being influenced by the tide.

In 1843, the same year in which Charles Dickens had written *A Christmas Carol*, the South Eastern Railway had opened their new harbour station in Folkestone. The company had realised that with the rapid expansion of the European rail networks and with the fashion for continental travel, it made good business sense to link the terminus at London Bridge to the coastal ports and take advantage of the well-established steamer services to Calais and Boulogne.

An act of Parliament authorising the South Eastern Railway was passed on 21 June 1836, but the company faced a difficult decision when choosing the best route, for James Abercrombie, the Speaker of the House of Commons, ruled that no further pathways out of London would be permitted. If the new company wished to link London to Dover it would have to use an existing route from the capital. The choice was between the lines operated by the London and Greenwich Railway to the East (the favoured route of William Cubitt who was the chief engineer for both companies) and the London and Brighton Railway to the west. The former route would have passed through Gravesend and Rochester and was the most direct, but the plan was blocked by the Admiralty. A complicated financial agreement was thus arranged with L&BR to share the tracks as far as Reigate, from where a new line was built heading eastwards through the Weald to Tonbridge, Paddock Wood and Ashford before cutting through the chalk cliffs and arriving at Folkestone. This arrangement explains the rather curious two-sides-of-triangle nature of the journey from London Bridge to the coast.

At that time Dover was the more established port, so the decision was made to embark upon a major civil engineering project to extend the line further east, which necessitated boring three tunnels: the Martello, Abbot's Cliff and Shakespeare.

Map showing the SERC route from London to Dover

Remarkably, the works came in not only on time but below budget too, and so it was that Dover and Folkestone became connected with London. The service was competitive, for the fare on a stagecoach (following the route from Dover to London that Dickens so memorably described in the opening chapter of *A Tale of Two Cities*) had been 30 shillings for an inside seat and 16 for an outside one. The first-class rail fare was only fifteen shillings. The company ran six trains in each direction every day and the service took slightly less than three hours.

Dover to Calais is the shortest route across the English Channel and therefore was the one most favoured by passengers who wanted to travel to Paris and beyond, so whilst it was Dover that grew as a passenger port, Folkestone carved its own niche.

In 1844 the mails from India were carried via river and coach to Boulogne and from there were transferred to the steam packets. At Folkestone crowds would gather at the harbour to watch the arrival of the ships, and the mail being transferred to the Folkestone Junction station to the north-east of the town, some distance from the quayside. Soon the little fishing village began to flourish.

During the 19th century the streets of Folkestone rose from the quayside up narrow cobbled streets towards more elegant residences overlooking the sea, and it seemed to be a topographical mirror to Boulogne just thirty miles away. Folkestone wasn't as grand as its French cousin and didn't boast huge cathedrals and monumental columns on its skyline, but the bustle of fishermen and shipping at the docks was the same.

Charles Dickens had stayed in Folkestone for three months in 1855, basing himself at 3 Albion Villas from where he had a commanding view not only of the sea, but also of the harbour railway station.

3 Albion Villas today

It was here that he began work on a new novel, *Little Dorrit*, which opens with Arthur Clenham returning from France to England:

'And thus ever by day and night, under the sun and under the stars, climbing the dusty hills and toiling along the weary plains, journeying by land and journeying by sea, coming and going so strangely, to meet and to act and react on one another, move all we restless travellers through the pilgrimage of life.'

As ever his correspondence was mainly work related, and he was constantly in touch with his office in London making sure that each edition of *Household Words* was perfectly put together. But there was other business that was even more important to him, personal business, for it was during his stay in Folkestone that he instructed Wills to begin negotiations for the purchase of Gad's Hill Place, the house he had first seen as a nine-year-old boy, a scene that he would retell in *The Uncommercial Traveller*:

'So smooth was the old high road, and so fresh were the horses, and so fast went I, that it was midway between Gravesend and Rochester, and the widening river was bearing the ships, white sailed or black-smoked, out to sea, when I noticed by the wayside a very queer small boy.

'"Holloa!" said I, to the very queer small boy, "where do you live?" "At Chatham," says he.

'"What do you do there?" says I. "I go to school," says he.

'I took him up in a moment, and we went on. Presently, the very queer small boy says, "This is Gad's Hill we are coming to, where Falstaff went out to rob those travellers, and ran away."

'"You know something about Falstaff, eh?" said I.

'"All about him," said the very queer small boy. "I am old (I am nine), and I read all sorts of books. But DO let us stop at the top of the hill, and look at the house there, if you please!" "You admire that house?" said I.

'"Bless you, sir," said the very queer small boy, "when I was not more than half as old as nine, it used to be a treat for me to be brought to look at it. And now, I am nine, I come by myself to look at it. And ever since I can recollect, my father, seeing me so fond of it, has often said to me, 'If you were to be very persevering and were to work hard, you might some day come to live in it.' Though that's impossible!" said the very queer small boy, drawing a low breath, and now staring at the house out of window with all his might.'

Dickens had dreamed of owning Gad's Hill Place throughout his childhood and now, at the age of 43, his father's prophecy was on the point of coming true.

He must have been thinking about his father a great deal during these weeks, for the early scenes of his new book were set in the Marshalsea Debtor's Prison and featured an independently minded child visiting her own father who was incarcerated there. These passages of *Little Dorrit* are among the most autobiographical fragments of his work.

Wherever he stayed Dickens loved to walk and during his time in Folkestone he spent many happy hours in the countryside lost in his own thoughts. In August he wrote to Frank Beard, his doctor, to reassure him that he was leading a healthy lifestyle: 'The Down-Lands in this neighbourhood — principally consisting of a chain of grass-covered hills of considerable elevation — are enchantingly fresh and free.'

The harbour at Folkestone was initially a simple stone affair with a long curving breakwater to protect the entrance. The coastal side of the harbour was known as The Stade whilst on the seaward wall was the South Pier. With the coming of the railway a small extra pier was built which would eventually extend across the harbour by means of a swing bridge to link with the South Pier and so lead to the creation of the Harbour Station.

As the land was actually owned by the railway company, and both rail and sea services were operated by them, it meant that they could plan and build facilities that would rival and surpass those at Dover. The platform was covered, there was a passenger terminal and an imposing customs house was soon built on the dock and soon Folkestone Harbour became the main station in the town, the Junction being much more inconveniently situated at the top of a steep hill, requiring an awkward and uncomfortable cab ride for the weary passengers.

Initially the harbour had allowed ships to dock with no

tidal restrictions, but with the coming of the larger ships such as the *Victoria* with their larger draft it became necessary to construct the New Pier. Although it was laudable to go to such lengths to ensure that the tides didn't affect the timing of the arrivals or departures, the fact that the port at Boulogne was tidal meant that there was still a necessary variation in the timetables.

Folkestone Harbour with The Victoria waiting to sail in the background, the rail platform alongside her.

Variations could be huge; we have already learned that on June 9th 1865 the tidal train was due to depart a full two hours earlier than it would on the following day, June 10th.

The passengers once more gathered their belongings, Dickens ensuring that the manuscript of *Our Mutual Friend* was safely in his pocket, and prepared to disembark onto the exposed pier from where there was just a short walk to the platform where the carriages that would carry them through the hop fields of Kent and into London waited. He bade farewell to Mr Melville, the librarian, no doubt making arrangements to meet in London as the porters and guards bustled about, loading the luggage and guiding the passengers to their various compartments alongside the curving platform.

At the head of the train were two small tank engines, with another at the rear, which would haul and push the heavy load up the long 1:30 gradient which linked the harbour to where the locomotive waited in a siding at Folkestone Junction.

The timetable stated that the departure would be at 2:36 and just two minutes late the tank engines started to take the strain, the couplings rattled as one after the other took up the slack in a series of little lurches, and so the journey began in a somewhat ignominious manner.

From the long platform the train rumbled past the signal box to the left and over the great iron swing bridge and timber viaduct. Fishing boats with their simple rigging were tethered in the inner harbour, safe from the elements, although on that the day the conditions were perfect. Far to the right the great stone cliffs towards Dover gleamed defiantly across the sea.

Once at the Junction the tank engines were uncoupled and the engine that would pull the train into London was carefully reversed into place and the couplings secured.

The locomotive, number 199, was an F class 'Dover Mail Single' which had a 2-2-2 configuration, meaning that there were two leading wheels on the front axle, two driving wheels which had a diameter of seven feet, and two trailing wheels. The fact that only the centre wheels drove and because of their size delivered great torque, was the reason that 199 was incapable of bringing the train up the hill from the harbour. Once on the flat, however, the huge driving wheel acted as a giant gear which created easy speed without using too much power. The cab and tender were painted in the dark green livery of the South Eastern Railway Company and had been built in the Ashford works to a design originally by James Cudworth, the Locomotive Superintendent of the South Eastern Railway Company. The design was a relatively recent one, having first come into service in 1861.

A 2-2-2 Single Locomotive of similar design to 199, with the tender carrying coal and water behind

Behind the locomotive was a tender carrying coal in the centre and a steam engine's life blood, water, in the surrounding tanks. Behind the tender was now attached a guard's van and behind that the first passenger carriage — a second class one, to which was coupled the first-class carriage in which Charles Dickens would be travelling.

The carriages each had four wheels and were made up of three self-contained compartments. They looked slightly ungainly atop the rails, almost as if they were part of a toy train set. In all there were ten passenger carriages, of which seven were first class and three second class. There were four further vans at the rear carrying the luggage and mail.

Besides the engineer George Crombie and his fireman William Beattie in the locomotive, there were three guards on the train. Lawrence Mercer was in the first van, and the other in two of the rearward ones. The latter guards had braking systems which operated on their own wagons, but of course they had no direct communication with the driver, other than the ability to sound the train's whistle to attract his attention. The first guard's van, behind the tender, was fitted with a Cremar's Patent Braking System which operated on two of the passenger carriages, as well as having his own standard braking system in his truck. In all five out of the fourteen vehicles had a braking system operating on them, although the standard systems were purely mechanical, using wooden shoes which had only a limited effect.

Crombie shifted the drive selector to the forward position and heaved the huge regulator lever to the left so that the steam could be forced into the cylinders where the pistons eased the connecting rods forward and turned the wheels. The locomotive shuddered slightly as the immense latent power was gradually released and slowly the tidal train left the platform behind it. In their first-class compartment Dickens and the Ternans settled into their seats for the last part of their journey. Charles had removed his greatcoat, complete with the precious manuscript, and hung it carefully.

In other coaches, behind the one occupied by Charles Dickens, Amelia Rayner sat with her son Lloyd and her sister-in-law. She had been born in New Brunswick and was well used to travel but her son was wide-eyed with excitement. Emma Beaumont, Caroline White, James Dunn, and many others hung their coats or shawls, stored their bags and parasols, gazed out of the windows and prepared for their journey through the Kentish hop fields.

Annie and Frederick Bodenham sat close together, lost in the excitement of their new life together, planning their future. Annie was 28 years old, Frederick 29.

Elsewhere Mrs Clodas was travelling with her six-year-old daughter, two other ladies and her brother-in-law. All the adults would have been making a fuss of the child who must have been terrified at the noise and speed of the train. No doubt the mother bounced the little girl on her lap to distract her.

In another compartment Mr Edward Dickenson, a young man destined for a career in the army, sat with Monsieur Mercier, a French cook, who, being in the employment of Admiral Fremantle from Devonport, spoke good English. The two exchanged pleasantries and then occupied themselves with their own thoughts. M. Mercier was looking forward to meeting friends in London and had written to them a few days earlier telling them to expect him at London Bridge on Friday afternoon.

Mr Dickenson was reading the newspaper accounts of the great and terrible rail crash which had taken place at Rednal near Shrewsbury the day before, the second that had befallen the Great Western Railway in recent days. An excursion from Chester had become derailed over a faulty stretch of line killing many passengers. As the train picked up speed, did Dickenson have a premonition of his own fate?

Riding in another of the plush first-class carriages were Martin Condliff and his wife Hannah. Martin was a gentleman of some importance, being not only a hotel keeper by trade but also the Mayor of his home town of Waterloo on the northern banks of the River Mersey. Hannah, a rather stout lady, was elegantly dressed in a black dress with red stripes.

Rattling, rocking, swaying, the train steamed through gently undulating hills criss-crossed with fields among the scattered farmhouses. Once through the Sandling tunnel and past Ashford station the landscape flattened out, with the ridge of the North Downs visible in the distance to the right, and featureless farmland to the left, although the view was occasionally obscured as the steam blew back along the sides of the carriages in the slipstream of the speeding express. Even with the windows closed the musty damp smell of steam permeated each compartment, especially those towards the front of the train. On the footplate Crombie kept the speed at a steady 50 miles an hour as the train rushed through Pluckley and on towards Headcorn.

Staplehurst: The Crash

The work over the Beult was progressing well and there was nothing to suggest that anything was amiss.

The final viaduct, nearest to Staplehurst, was constructed on brick piers and spanned 168 feet over eight arches of 21 feet each. The word viaduct suggests a monumental structure spanning a great chasm, but the bridges over the Beult were only ten feet above the river. During the summer of '65 the river was little more than a muddy stream, although during the winter months it would flood the entire basin beneath the arches. On top of the brickwork were longitudinal cast-iron girders with troughs set into the top and it was in these troughs that the wooden baulks lay. On top of the baulks the rails would be fitted.

Two of the three rotten baulks had already been replaced and the rails over them re-laid successfully, meaning there was only one stretch left to be completed. Two lengths of rail, each of twenty-one feet long, had been removed; a thirteen-foot length of new timber, with the rail already in place on it, lay next to the viaduct waiting to be lifted into the girders.

Henry Benge continued to lead his team well and they continued to follow his direction as they had dutifully for ten weeks.

It was three o'clock in the afternoon, and 544 yards away John Wiles sat in boredom waiting for the apparently interminable day to end. Next to him on the ground lay the two unplaced explosive warning charges and his red flag. It was a warm day and no doubt he was occasionally nodding off.

At eleven minutes past three it was reported that the tidal train passed through Headcorn station (still running two minutes late, according to the timetable), and it was travelling at full steam, as befitted one of the rail company's blue riband services. George Crombie kept his eye on the way ahead, the regulator only slightly open now, enough to maintain speed but not so much as to drain the tanks of precious water, for there would be no stops during this journey to refill the tender. The fireman William Beattie made sure that the furnace burned well and shovelled more coal as necessary. He also kept an eagle eye on the water gauges so that as soon as the levels dropped, he could open the valves to allow more to flow into the boiler from the tender. It was also the fireman's duty to keep a look out for any danger if, as the regulations stated, he was 'not otherwise engaged'.

In Edward Dickenson's compartment the French passenger Hippolite Mercier asked if they might change places, as he didn't like the wind rushing in at the window. Dickenson agreed and the two gentlemen swapped their seats. This apparently inconsequential exchange saved Mr Dickenson's life.

The stretch of line from Headcorn to Staplehurst is absolutely straight and there is no gradient to speak of. Despite the fact that it pulled fourteen loaded carriages and vans the locomotive was travelling at its top speed of fifty miles per hour as it approached Sloman's Crossing, the small bridge linking two halves of a local farmer's fields. Here some men were working the land and paused in their labours to watch the express thunder past.

What was it that first roused the labourer Wiles from his torpor? Did he hear the rails singing? Was there, as Dickens would write a year later in his ghost story *The Signalman*, 'a vague vibration in the earth and air, quickly changing into a violent pulsation, and an oncoming rush that caused me to start back'? Maybe he didn't fully register the import of the situation for a few seconds, but the sound of an express train at full speed would have been completely different to that which he had heard when the local train had rumbled along the line earlier in the afternoon. Leaping up Wiles grabbed his flag and waved it wildly.

At the viaduct the working crew would have felt and heard the vibration in the rails too, especially as the ends were free. Edward Coleman, one of the carpenters, looked to Benge for advice, who simply exclaimed, 'Oh dear! Here's the boat train — what shall we do?'

Benge, Coleman, Dawson and other members of the team ran up the track waving their arms 'making', as Coleman stated, 'all the signs we could to stop the train'.

On the footplate George Crombie was aware of something out of the ordinary in the periphery of his vision and had noticed the rapid flurry of red as he sped by. If the explosive charges had been placed according to the regulations, then two would have gone off thereby instantly alerting the three guards of danger meaning they could have applied their brakes straight away. As it was only the driver knew of the danger and he reacted exactly as he should have done, but with so little distance in which to stop the train he had no chance. The engine had travelled forty-four yards before the driver was able to take action, meaning it was still travelling at fifty miles an hour with only five hundred yards to go before the breach in the line. Initially he slammed the regulator shut, cutting off the supply of steam and then reached up for the cord above his head and sounded two short emergency calls on the whistle and it was only now that the guards realised that something was wrong. All three reached for their various braking systems.

In the cab, having sounded the whistle, Crombie applied his brakes, yanked the huge lever from its 'forward' position into reverse and opened the regulator for full steam again. The huge driving wheels began to spin backwards on the rails, emitting showers of sparks as they battled against forward momentum. In the leading guard's van Lawrence Mercer, reacting to the emergency whistles, applied the regular brake first, which cost a little more time, for the patent braking system which operated on the two leading passenger carriages (including the one in which Dickens was travelling), was designed to work instantly whereas the older standard brakes with their ineffectual wooden shoes took time to have any effect. The two rearward guards only had the regular brakes and were largely powerless in pulling the mighty express train to a halt.

At the official inquiry into the accident the driver would give evidence suggesting that he had managed to slow the train to a mere ten miles per hour, but with the distance travelled before the brakes were applied, as well as the ultimate state of the wreckage it seems more likely that the speed as the wheels reached the bridge was closer to 30 miles per hour.

There must have been a terrible sense of inevitability and hopelessness in the minds of Crombie, and Beattie on the footplate, and the same was surely true of Henry Benge and those working on his team as they leaped off the bridge and away from the scene. The temporary signalman John Wiles, his useless red flag still in his hand hanging limply by his side, watched the back of the last brake vans as it receded knowing that any moment there would be an explosion of noise and the calm peaceful scene of the Kentish fields would be shattered.

Sitting in their carriages the various passengers would have lurched forward as the brakes were vigorously applied, and they would have heard the whistle crying, but they could have no idea what was about to befall them. Mrs Clodus held her child more closely, Frederick Bodenham placed a comforting arm around Annie, Charles Dickens looked up at Ellen, Amelia Rayner put a hand out to steady herself and grasped the seat.

In the cab the driver's knuckles were white with gripping the regulator lever, as if that would make any difference, and the noise of the engine at full steam, accompanied by the shriek and squeal of the wheels spinning backwards on the iron rails filled his ears. Maybe he had his hand on the whistle which sounded less of a warning now but more of a wail of death in harmony with the screams of terror from him and his fireman. The wheels ran off the end of the rails, but fortunately remained in the troughs of the girders, thereby maintaining the semblance of a straight course.

At 3:13 the locomotive's front wheels met fresh air.

It is a strange quirk of circumstance that the very issue that led to the crash, that is George Crombie's inability to lose more speed, actually saved the life of Charles Dickens on June 9th, 1865.

The locomotive, with the weight of the heavy tender forcing it on, had so much momentum that it actually managed to jump the gap in the rails, pulling with it not only the tender but the guard van, and the second-class carriage as well. The engine remained upright with its right-hand wheels between the rails on the other side of the bridge and the left wheels between the rail and a fence. The rails in place on the Staplehurst side of the bridge were ripped up and twisted by the impact and the iron girders were also contorted from the violence of the crash.

The locomotive travelled a further 28 feet before finally coming to a rest. The tender was still attached to it but had slewed through 90 degrees and had come to rest across the line. The van behind had become uncoupled and also lay across the lines but in the opposite direction to the tender. Somehow the coupling linking the guard's van to the second-class carriage was not broken and the latter vehicle sat straight on the viaduct with its rear wheels dangling in mid-air looking like a gibbet to the hanging corpse of the first-class carriage behind, the rear of which rested lightly on the muddy riverbed below.

It was in this carriage that Charles Dickens and his companions lay in a corner of their compartment, where they had been flung together.

The rest of the carriages had plunged off the bridge, each crushing the one in front. The first-class carriage immediately following Dickens' had fallen onto its roof and the flimsy wooden chassis was flattened by the heavy iron wheels of the following cars piling onto it. The lucky passengers, such as Frederick Bodenham and Edward Dickenson, were flung out of the carriages as they lurched into the river and lay dazed in the mud and water of the riverbed. As the windows and wooden panels were smashed so deadly shards sliced indiscriminately through the air, burying themselves in whatever, or whoever, was in their way.

Much of our knowledge of the accident comes from Charles Dickens himself in the form of a letter that he wrote a few days later to his friend Thomas Mitton and that letter deserves to be reproduced in its entirety:

GAD'S HILL PLACE, HIGHAM BY ROCHESTER, KENT.
Tuesday, Thirteenth June 1865

My Dear Mitton.

I should have written to you yesterday or the day before, if I had been quite up to writing. I am a *little* shaken, not by the beating and dragging of the carriage in which I was, but by the hard work afterwards in getting out the dying and dead, which was most horrible.

I was in the only carriage that did not go over into the stream. It was caught upon the turn by some of the ruin of the bridge and hung suspended and balanced in an apparently impossible manner. Two ladies were my fellow passengers; an old one, and a young one. This is exactly what passed: you may judge from it the precise length of the suspense. Suddenly we were off the rail and beating the ground as the car of a half-emptied balloon might. The old lady cried out 'My God!' and the young one screamed. I caught hold of them both (the old lady sat opposite, and the young one on my left), and said: 'We can't help ourselves, but we can be quiet and composed. Pray don't cry out.' The old lady immediately answered, 'Thank you. Rely upon me. Upon my soul, I will be quiet.' The young lady said in a frantic way, 'Let us join hands and die friends.' We were then all tilted down together in a corner of the carriage and stopped. I said to them thereupon: 'You may be sure nothing worse can happen. Our danger *must* be over. Will you remain here without stirring, while I get out of the window?' They both answered quite collectedly, 'Yes,' and I got out without the least notion what had happened.

Fortunately, I got out with great caution and stood upon the step. Looking down, I saw the bridge gone and nothing below me but the line of rail. Some people in the two other compartments were madly trying to plunge out at window and had no idea that there was an open swampy field 15 feet down below them and nothing else! The two guards (one with his face cut) were running up and down on the down side of the bridge (which was not torn up) quite wildly. I called out to them, 'Look at me. Do stop an instant and look at me, and tell me whether you don't know me.' One of them answered, 'We know you very well, Mr. Dickens.' 'Then,' I said, 'my good fellow, for God's sake give me your key, and send one of those labourers here, and I'll empty this carriage.' — We did it quite safely, by means of a plank or two, and when it was done, I saw all the rest of the train except the two baggage cars down in the stream. I got into the carriage again for my brandy flask, took off my travelling hat for a basin, climbed down the brickwork, and filled my hat with water.

Suddenly I came upon a staggering man covered with blood (I think he must have been flung clean out of his carriage) with such a frightful cut across the skull that I couldn't bear to look at him. I poured some water over his face, and gave him some to drink, and gave him some brandy, and laid him down on the grass, and he said 'I am gone' and died afterwards. Then I stumbled over a lady lying on her back against a little pollard tree, with the blood streaming over her face (which was lead colour) in a number of distinct little streams from the head. I asked her if she could swallow a little brandy, and she just nodded, and I gave her some and left her for somebody else. The next time I passed her, she was dead. Then a man examined at the Inquest yesterday (who evidently had not the least remembrance of what really passed) came running up to me and implored me to help him find his wife, who was afterwards found dead. No imagination can conceive the ruin of the carriages, or the extraordinary weights under which the people were lying, or the complications into which they were twisted up among iron and wood, and mud and water.

I don't want to be examined at the Inquest, and I don't want to write about it. It could do no good either way, and I could only seem to speak about myself, which, of course I would rather not do. I am keeping very quiet here. I have a — I don't know what to call it — constitutional (I suppose) presence of mind and was not in the least fluttered at the time. I instantly remembered that I had the MS. of a No. with me and clambered back into the carriage for it. But in writing these scanty words of recollection I feel the shake and am obliged to stop.

Ever faithfully, C.D.

Within the letter there are some interesting points, which help to build the picture of the day, firstly Charles's extreme calmness despite the violence and suddenness of the crash. Immediately the initial panic was over he took it upon himself to calm the ladies, imploring them not to cry or shout out lest they should alarm other passengers. Another moment of note is the fact that Ellen seemed to want to effect some kind of reconciliation, as she rather theatrically pleaded that they

'...join hands and die friends', which seems to suggest that there had been a disagreement or a sense of awkwardness between them during the journey. Dickens did not react to Ellen's request specifically, at least he didn't tell Mitton that he did, but instead, having ascertained that they were in no further danger assisted them from their compartment, along with other passengers in the carriage, with the help of the railway staff. What happened to the Ternans for the rest of the day is not known.

Staplehurst: The Rescue

Another account which was published in the sensational newspaper reports of the time confirms Dickens' observations:

'About 45 minutes after leaving Folkestone, which we did within two minutes of the hour appointed — 2:30 — I became sensible of some impending danger, as the brakes were applied most vigorously, accompanied by that hoarse staccato note of the brake whistle which is so ominous a sound to those who know its significance. Within twenty seconds the train made a sudden jump and it became instantly apparent that we were off the metals. The next few seconds of dread and uncertainty is impossible to describe. The rush of blood to the heart and the brain on the certain conviction that a fearful crisis is imminent has probably been experienced by all who have reached the age of 25, or even fewer years, but in this instance was aggravated by the jolting and plunging of the carriage which was terrific.

'When the train came to a standstill and I got out of the window, the door of course being locked, the first thing that arrested my attention was the wonderful position of the carriage which I had just left. The front wheel was completely off the line in mid-air, the hind wheel had been arrested by the girder of the bridge on which the catastrophe occurred, and had the carriage been propelled another yard it must inevitably been turned over like the rest, only probably with consequences, if possible, more disastrous, as the ground underneath was much harder than where the others fell.

'The scene from the bridge baffles all description. Eight or nine first-class carriages had been turned over and smashed into an almost undistinguishable mass of ruins. Indeed, where I stood and looked down upon the splintered fragments it was impossible to tell how many carriages were there. But for some minutes there was no noise: no human voice raised. The worst had come and was past; there was nothing more to fear.

'Some few had been struck down at a blow; some were crushed and unconscious, and probably before consciousness returned, had died of suffocation in the twelve or fourteen inches of mud and water into which several of the carriages had been thrown. Some were crawling out of the ruins, half stunned, bleeding and mutilated in different degrees, but for some minutes the silence was appalling.'

From the fact that Charles Dickens stated that he 'saw all the rest of the train except the two baggage cars down in the stream' it must be assumed that this second account was given by one of the rear guards, and his precise knowledge of the train's departure time from Folkestone as well as his reaction to the ominous whistle confirms this assumption.

On the other side of the bridge at the front of the train Dickens now surveyed the scene before him and the adrenaline must have been coursing through his veins, for this was the man who just a few days earlier had been complaining about his swollen left leg, and who had been on the point of breaking down. Now he clambered down the little bank into the heart of the wreck.

The full horror began to impress itself upon Dickens' mind, but he worked diligently and with great compassion tending anyone he came across with his flask and improvised water vessel.

In his efforts he was helped by the crew of the train, all of whom survived (the driver, fireman and the first guard had been in vehicles that had safely cleared the gap, whilst the remaining two guards, including the author of the account above, were in the rear baggage vans that stopped before they fell into the river), and by members of Henry Benge's working team.

After the initial moments of shocked silence, the noise became awful with the air filled with screams of pain from the wounded and cries of anguish from those who searched for their loved ones among the twisted metal and shattered shards of wood. The river, little more than a stream at that time of year, and from which Dickens tried to scoop cooling water, had been polluted with oil, coal and blood. The furnace in the locomotive still burned red hot, although thankfully it was on the viaduct well clear of the main wreckage and did not endanger those who were trapped or those who tried to help them.

Five years later Charles Dickens would describe the Kentish countryside at this time of year in his final novel *The Mystery of Edwin Drood*: '…rich trees waving in the balmy air, changes of glorious light from the moving boughs, songs of birds, scents of gardens, woods and fields, or rather the one great garden of the whole cultivated island….'; what a vast contrast between his idyll of a peaceful, sunny bucolic scene and the hellish assault on the senses that he experienced in 1865.

As Charles clambered into the river, amongst the wreckage, his only thoughts were to help the wounded and what a helpless task faced him. He called to his fellow rescuers that he had brandy, although one in the confusion thought that he was asking for some and called back that there was none to be had. Dickens ran from one person to another, comforting them and allowing them to drink as he cradled them in his arms.

Elsewhere Mrs Clodas pulled herself from the mud, with the help of her brother-in-law and instantly began to cry out for her daughter who had been sitting on her lap before their carriage fell into the river. Who can imagine the extraordinary extremes of emotions, panic first and then utter relief when they heard a little girl crying? Mr Clodas stumbled and splashed through the mire to assist and together they managed to pull the child to safety. Amazingly, none of the party were physically injured and they sat on the little grass bank holding one another crying tears of relief. By this time more people were arriving at the scene to assist, and the Clodas family were gently led away to the nearby Spring Hill Farm where they were looked after by the farmer Mr Ebenezer Ballard and his wife Charlotte. 'Being completely saturated and disfigured with mud and slime they were supplied with fresh clothes,' reported the *Dundee Courier and Argus*.

Charles Dickens, already having witnessed the death of two

people that he had tried to help, now came across the inert body of Mr Dickenson trapped in a dark void. A sense of despair and helplessness came over him until suddenly Dickenson choked and moaned. With the aid of a labourer Charles managed to pull the figure out from beneath the remains of the carriage and proceeded to offer him brandy. Dickenson was '…bleeding at the eyes, ears, nose, and mouth; but didn't seem to know that afterwards, and of course I didn't tell him'. The warming spirit touched his lips and Mr Dickenson began to revive. 'If I hadn't had the brandy to give him at the moment, I think he would have been done for… he was the first person whom the brandy saved.'

Another survivor also found himself among the wreckage and recalled the harrowing scenes that he saw:

'Just as the train arrived at Staplehurst and while I was reading the severe comments in one of the morning papers on the railway accident in Shrewsbury, I and my fellow passengers were startled by a deep and heavy sounding noise; then followed two terrible jolts or bumps, and, in an instant afterwards, from bright sunshine all became darkness.

'In a second or two I found myself enveloped in moisture and then in the terrible din I became conscious that an accident had happened to the train in which I was a passenger. I found myself afterwards up to my knees in water, and in the middle of a heap of broken carriages, amidst which the whole of the party I had seen but a short time ago on board the steamer, were lying.

'The carriages, with one exception, I now discovered had been thrown from the bridge over which the trains pass at Staplehurst into the water below and death and destruction reigned around.

'The remains of the shattered carriages were projecting wheels upwards from the water, and the screams of the sufferers were heartrending. Immediately I could relieve myself from the perilous position I, with some other gentlemen who fortunately escaped with a few bruises and a plunge in the water, endeavoured to extricate some of our less fortunate fellow passengers.

'We succeeded, after great difficulty, in getting a female from the muddy bed of the river, all but dead, and as we were assisting another sufferer, Mr Charles Dickens, who was a passenger, came upon the scene. He, it appeared, had occupied a seat in the only carriage that did not go over the bridge, although the chance that it did not do so was the slightest in the world. This carriage, which was the first from the engine, had held firm by the coupling iron to the tender, and thus it was prevented from sharing the fate of the others, although it literally hung half upon the line, half down the bank, and high above the terrible confusion below.

'Mr Dickens was most energetic in the assistance he rendered to his fellow passengers. I heard this gentleman call for some brandy for some of the wounded persons, but unfortunately none was at hand, it being with the luggage, or else in the possession of those who were struggling in the river. As brandy was not to be had, Charles Dickens took off his hat, and having filled it with water, I saw him running about with it and doing his best to revive and comfort every poor creature he met who had sustained serious injury.

'Another gentleman, who I found afterwards to be Mr Samuel Reed, a gentleman connected with *The Illustrated London News,* acted in a praiseworthy manner, for although he had a narrow escape from a terrible death, he with great nerve assisted in extricating those imploring help from beneath the carriages.

'One lady whom I had particularly noticed on board the steamer as being a very fine and handsome person I saw taken from the water; she had actually been crushed to death, and as she was laid out on the bank, her husband, who had been previously frantically about exclaiming "My wife! My wife!" came up, and when he discovered that the mangled and disfigured corpse was that of her, he sat down by the body, a figure of utter despair.

'I cannot dwell upon this terrible scene. It is too much for human nature.'

Was the man who Dickens described as coming 'running up to me and implored me to help him find his wife' and who the other correspondent had heard crying 'My wife! My wife!' Frederick Bodenham? It seems likely, for his new bride Annie was another of the victims in the crash. Their life together in Hereford, he as a respected solicitor with a beautiful young wife to keep his house, had been ripped from them and Annie lay dead on the riverbank as Frederick wept. Just a few minutes before they had sat together in the safety of their compartment, but at the moment that the carriage lurched into the river Frederick was thrown clear and into the water. Annie was not so fortunate.

Of course, the agitated gentleman could have been the Merseyside hotel keeper and town mayor Martin Condliff, for he was reported to be making urgent enquiries about the whereabouts of his wife and telling anyone he came across about her black and red striped dress.

Also, within the wreck lay the crushed and contorted dead body of Hyppolite Mercier, the French chef who only a few minutes earlier had politely asked if he might change seats.

According to Dickens he stayed in the river tending the injured for two to three hours and what he witnessed there shocked him profoundly. In a letter to Angela Burdett-Coutts he said that 'I worked hard afterwards among the dead and dying, and it is that shock — not the shock of the stumbling carriage, which was nothing — that I feel a little. I could not have imagined so appalling a scene.'

As we have heard Charles Dickens was not the only passenger to assist in the rescue attempt, for the human spirit is such that everyone who was physically able did everything that they could. *The Bolton Chronicle* reported that 'those of the passengers who escaped injury in the first instance behaved nobly towards their fellows in distress. There was no standing irresolute on the bank: everything that willing hands could do was done at once.'

As soon as the severity of the crash became apparent a telegram was dispatched to London Bridge which baldly stated that several passengers had been killed and many wounded' The Telegram arrived at 3.30, only fifteen minutes after the accident had occurred. On receipt of the terrible news the railway company immediately dispatched a train from London Bridge carrying not only Cornelius Eborall, the general manager of South Eastern Railways, and the traffic superintendent Mr Knight, but also such medical help that could be roused at so short a notice, including Doctors Jones, Adams and Palfrey. At Guys Hospital, which is located near to London Bridge station, a hundred beds were prepared for the injured. Locally doctors were also called from the towns of Tonbridge and Ashford and soon there were more than 20 medically trained personnel working to stabilise the condition of the survivors. Some were carried into the shadows of the nearby trees to keep the hot sun off them but as Dickens mournfully noted the shade soon had 'as many dead in it as living'

At nearby Staplehurst Place the family of respected banker Henry Hoare provided a carriage so that the most severely injured could be quickly moved away from the scene and treated in relative comfort. The Hoare family knew only too well the importance of swift intervention, for Henry, a senior partner in C. Hoare and Company the family owned private bank, had suffered serious and ultimately mortal injuries in a train accident just two months earlier when he leaned out of a carriage window as his train past a bridge parapet.

Even as the rescue efforts continued, so the investigations as to the cause of the catastrophe began and even at that early stage there was little doubt as to where the blame lay. The guard from the rear brake van was vehemently angry about the circumstances:

'It is a total misapplication of the term to call what happened on Friday an accident. It is no more an accident than it would be an accident if a paviour dug a pitfall in Piccadilly and no light was placed to warn the public that it had been made.

'The cause of the catastrophe, as related to me by the driver of the engine, is simply this, that the platelayers had taken up one if not two plates, and the only warning they gave him that the line of rail was thus disturbed was by sending a man about 150 yards to meet the train with a red flag.'

As afternoon turned into evening David Ovenden, the Superintendent of the Kent County Constabulary, arrived to interview those most closely involved, and his suspicions quickly turned to Henry Benge whom he interrogated at the scene. The interview was not a long one:

'Well Benge, how did this happen?'

'Well, sir, I misread the timetable of Saturday for Friday.'

'Benge, you must consider yourself in custody, for I am going to take you on the charge of manslaughter of those persons who have been killed.'

Henry Benge, in shock, said nothing more than, 'It is a sad business.'

Ovenden searched his prisoner and found the timetable book which had been so disastrously misread at breakfast. The fact that by this time Henry was aware that he had mistaken Friday's timetable for Saturday's means that even as the dead and wounded were removed from the wreck, he had been reading the book over and over again to try and understand what had happened.

Most of the victims were identified at the scene by travelling companions and loved ones but three bodies remained anonymous for a while. One woman was quickly identified as Hannah Condliff thanks to her name being embroidered into her garments and by the description of her black and red dress given by her agitated husband, who himself was beginning to suffer from the injuries that he had received in the crash. Another victim was a man whose injuries were so severe that identification was impossible. His socks were marked with the initials 'HM', and in his pocket a letter was found with the address 'M Leon, 6 Rutland Terrace, Thames Bank, Pimilico'. Another lady had nothing on her person to specifically identify her but a letter sent from the city of Lincoln bearing the name Beaumont addressed to 11 Rue de Challot, Champs-Elysées, Paris.

Although most of the rescuers who arrived assisted in removing debris and pulling passengers to safety, the local school master with the splendidly Pickwickian name of Sidney Samuel Simkin made it his role to document everybody's name, home address and condition.

Among the crowds that gathered to mawkishly survey the scene was the local hairdresser Frederick Watson who was beginning to embrace the new art of photography. Hurriedly he set up his bulky equipment and laboriously exposed three glass plates before the chemicals dried. In front of him the carriage in which Dickens had ridden had been lifted back onto the track where it stood forlornly as if it were the sole survivor of an apocalypse.

In the wreckage and under the shade of the trees that had become the alfresco mortuary Charles Dickens gave all the help that he could, but after three hours there was little left to do. By this time that initial surge of adrenaline had worn off and the body, so frail but a few days before, became exhausted once more. He stood and sorrowfully surveyed the scene before him. By this time trains which had been sent from

London Bridge to ferry the wounded back to London were making frequent trips and Charles was convinced to return to the metropolis.

Despite the shock of the afternoon's events there was still a clarity in the great man's mind and before making his way to the waiting train that would remove him from the nightmare, he clambered back up the bank to the plank that had been his exit bridge from his own compartment. Still hanging on the hook was his greatcoat and, in the pocket, the unharmed manuscript of *Our Mutual Friend*, which he retrieved.

Charles now allowed himself to be led towards Staplehurst station and there he climbed into a carriage where he found himself in the company of Edward Dickenson, the man whom he had pulled from the wreckage and comforted with brandy. The marks of dried blood covered Dickenson's face and clothes but he refused to believe that he was seriously injured, despite Charles's protestations to the contrary.

The Aftermath

One can only imagine how the battered, dirty and broken passengers felt as they heard a whistle blow and felt the carriage lurch. Were there shouts of fear? Gripping of seats? Eyes wide as the horror of the afternoon came back to them once more? Or was physical and emotional exhaustion so complete that the gentle rocking of the train cossetted and comforted them as they were carried away from the horror of a Kentish field and back to the reality of a busy city?

At Charing Cross the stationmaster Mr Dyne was busying himself giving journalists and inquisitive members of the public as much information as he could, as well as meeting each of the trains that carried the wounded. Most of the passengers seemed disoriented and confused, displaying the unmistakable signs of shock but a few were able to go on their way without further medical assistance. One such was Mademoiselle Gouverneur who despite being shaken was able to take a cab to her home in Twickenham.

At the station a delirious woman gave her name as Miss Tipps but by the time she had been taken to Guy's Hospital she was calling herself Patterson. The injuries ranged from small abrasions and contusions to severe head injuries and broken limbs and many were taken to nearby hotels, as well as the hospital, to recover. A Mr Graham found himself at The St James' Hotel where he was treated for a fracture to his leg and a badly cut face, whilst Mr and Mrs Lord, both with serious injuries, were taken to The Castle and Falcon where they stayed until they were well enough to return to their home in Muckle Terrace, Bolton.

Meanwhile the journalists with their voracious appetites for a story began to build their pictures of what had occurred. The early editions printed on the 10th June had sketchy accounts of the crash, but with each passing day the descriptions became more detailed and an ever longer list of the dead and wounded was published ensuring that a more human tale could be told.

The *Sussex Advertiser* printed these details on June 13th:

'List of persons injured:

Major Francis. Thigh fractured. Left arm, eye, chin contused.

Mr Condriff. Right clavicle fractured, and severe concussion. Head and eye contused.

Mr Ralph. Ribs fractured.

Mrs Ralph. Contusion of head and legs.

Mr Hunt. Arm &tc fractured.

Miss Alexander. Scalp wound &tc.

Rev. Mr Eland. Left shoulder joint and legs damaged.

Mrs Eland. Fractured elbow and head contused.

Miss Eales. Bruised, not much hurt.

Miss Bertha Alleyne, left hip severely contused. Eye contused.

Mr Moss Defries, damage to left shoulder — suspected fracture scalp wound, and bruised knee.

Mr Lloyd Rayner, fracture of leg and scalp injured.

Miss Caroline Harmes, contused head and wrist.

Miss Kate Harmes, back contused, scalp wound and bruised shoulder.

Miss White, living in Pau and Brighton, bruised shoulder &tc.

Miss White, sister of Miss White at Mr May's, severe collapse, damage to head.

The sufferers according to the latest accounts are going on favourably.'

Other reports told of Mrs Hampson, the surgeon's wife from Bolton, being cut about the head, her husband being among the dead. Mr Hunt and Monsieur Le Marchant being 'considerably hurt and wrapped in bandages', and Mrs Ann Epps was taken to the Charing Cross Hospital. Frederick Bodenham, the solicitor from Hereford '...carried, half unconsciously, the bonnet worn by his wife on the journey that was so lamentably and, in her case, fatally interrupted.'

The reporters were diligent in their research and the list of individuals and their injuries was comprehensive and impressive, but from every account published there was one name missing: Ternan.

In the moments after the accident Charles Dickens had comforted his travelling companions but could see that Ellen was in distress and injured. She had been thrown into the corner of the carriage as it lurched down and now lay with cuts, bruises and probably a broken upper arm, injuries consistent with those suffered by the other passengers. The gold jewellery that Ellen travelled with was nowhere to be seen and had either been lost through the window or was somewhere in the upturned carriage.

Dickens had opened the window and called to the labourers, 'Look at me. Do stop an instant and look at me, and tell me whether you don't know me... my good fellow, for God's sake give me your key, and send one of those labourers here, I'll empty this carriage.' Thus he was able to get Ellen and Frances out of the train and to safety before anyone knew they were even there. When the ladies were out of the way Charles clambered back into the carriage to collect his bottle of brandy and from there made his way down to the riverbank where he began assisting in the rescue for which he has become so famous and which was immortalised by an engraving published on the front page of *The Penny Illustrated Paper*.

I do not suggest that Dickens' actions were a cynical ploy to divert attention from the identity of his travelling companions, but that is what was achieved, which was a coincidental and fortunate outcome for him.

Presumably the Ternans were taken from the scene, perhaps they were led away to Mr Ballard's farm with the Clodas family, where they waited for the first of the relief trains to take them to London and back to anonymity.

It was the early evening when Charles Dickens returned to the city. Mr Dickenson, his travelling companion, was taken to the Charing Cross Hospital, while Charles made his way to the offices of *All The Year Round* where he finally handed over the manuscript for the 16th monthly instalment of *Our Mutual Friend*.

Saturday, 10th June

On Saturday 10th June the newspapers were published and the accident at Staplehurst was a major story. Considering that there were still reports of the disaster at Rednal, another crash made for excellent copy and the new story had the advantage of celebrity involvement. Even at this early stage it was reported that Charles Dickens had been involved, and that gave the story a greater sense of import. *The Examiner* headlined the account simply 'Another Railway Accident. Ten Persons Killed — Upwards Of Twenty Wounded'. Having briefly described the circumstances of the accident the story went on to tell its readers that 'Mr Charles Dickens had a narrow escape. He was in the train, but, fortunately for himself and the interests of literature, received no injuries whatever.'

In the offices of *All The Year Round* the author began to write letters and the first was to his physician Doctor Frank Beard, and immediately the shock to his system was apparent:

My Dear Frank Beard

I was in the terrible accident yesterday and worked some hours among the dying and dead.

I was in the carriage that did not go down but hung in the air over the side of the broken bridge. I was not touched — scarcely shaken. But the terrific nature of the scene makes me think that I should be the better for a gentle composing draught or two.

I must away to Gad's directly to quiet their minds. John would get made and would bring down, any prescription you might let him have here. Don't come down to Gad's, yourself, unless you can stay all night and be comfortable. In that case, do.

Ever Yours CD.

(I can't sign my flourish to-day!)

He then pulled out another sheet of notepaper and wrote another letter and another and another, using the same phrases over and over again as a modern author might cut and paste a sentence.

The repetition was almost as if he were forcing himself to relive the terrible scenes; as if he were punishing himself for surviving when others had not.

To William Day he wrote: 'Tell Mr Clowes that I was not touched in the terrible railway accident yesterday. I was in the carriage that did not go over the bridge but hung suspended in the air. I was scarcely shaken, and able to work for hours among the dying and dead.'

To John Forster: 'I was in the terrific Staplehurst accident yesterday and worked for hours among the dying and dead. I was in the carriage that did not go over, but went off the line, and hung over the bridge in an inexplicable manner. No words can describe the scene. I am away to Gad's.'

To Charles Lever: 'I was in the frightful accident yesterday and worked for hours among the dying and dead. I was in the carriage that did not go down, but that hung inexplicably suspended in the air over the side of the broken bridge.'

To Frederick Ouvry: 'I was in the terrific accident yesterday (under-stated in the papers this morning) and worked for hours among the dying and dead. I was in the carriage that did not go over, and that hung inexplicably in the air over the side of the broken bridge. I am not touched — scarcely shaken.'

And so on.

It is clear that he was not severely affected by any physical trauma, or by the knowledge that he had escaped death so narrowly, but he was certainly profoundly disturbed by the scenes he had witnessed among the wreckage.

At some stage during the day he was able to visit Ellen, comforting and reassuring her. Her broken arm would need to be treated properly and there is no doubt that he would have contacted Doctor Beard to ask him to ensure that the finest treatment should be given to the patient.

He asked Ellen what she needed to be comfortable and promised that he would arrange for whatever she requested to be sent to her. It was during this time together that she told him that all the gold she had been carrying on the journey was missing. It was a feature of the crash that personal effects were ripped from the passengers (when recounting the story of Edward Dickenson's rescue Charles mentioned that 'in the moment of going over the viaduct, the whole of his pockets were shaken empty! He had no watch, no chain, no money, no pocketbook, no handkerchief, when we got him out'). Charles promised Ellen that he would make enquiries and it was this promise that brought the relationship between Charles Dickens and Ellen Ternan to the notice of a much wider audience than that of his immediate circle of friends.

During the Saturday the final relief trains returned from Staplehurst. Mr Eborall and Mr Knight of the railway company accompanied the final passengers, bandaged and bruised, to London. Some whose injuries were too severe to allow for travel remained in Staplehurst and the local community rallied around to help, offering their homes as hospital wards.

At Staplehurst Place the Hoare family, who earlier had loaned their carriage to assist in the rescue effort, now prepared the grand house to look after any victims who might need a bed. In her diary Caroline Hoare (a daughter of Henry and Mary) wrote 'We came home before long, leaving Charles to do what he could and bye and bye he came back for sheets and at last when we were at tea, he brought back a poor little fellow, Lloyd Rayner, whose leg was broken and who had lost his mother and whose Aunt was very badly hurt.' The Charles referred to in this entry was Caroline's younger brother.

The Hoares, or rather their household, were used to caring for children for there were twelve siblings in all, and Lloyd would probably have been under the loving supervision of Elizabeth Springatt, the governess. Lloyd would stay for over a month. He became popular with the family and Caroline expressed the sadness of the entire household when she recorded on 11th July that 'At 12 Dr. Willington came to escort Lloyd to London; all felt sorry to lose him and he very loath to go, poor boy; he went at 12½, having given Mama a very pretty kettle holder worked by himself.'

The Reverend Eland, the vicar of Bedminster and his wife were under the care of Doctor John Wilkins, along with their fellow passengers Mr de Fries, Bertha Alleyne and her companion Miss Eales.

Doctor Wilkin had been among the first men on the scene when he was told about the accident by a railway worker knocking at his door. He had arrived at the scene at around half-past three, just fifteen minutes after the crash, and had immediately tended the wounded and examined the bodies that had been already been removed. 'All the deaths were caused by the accident. I have seen six females and three males.'

In the Railway Station Hotel to the north of the town Martin Condliff lay, still desperate to find his wife in the black and red dress. Even the organised schoolmaster Mr Simkin was getting impatient, '...he seems to be complaining very much!'

The body of Caroline White was looked after in Miss May's house, while her cousin was tended by Richard Barnes and his family.

The Crown Hotel in nearby Cranbrook had become a temporary hospital where Monsieur Rousell and Charles Landour lay in the comfortable beds, both suffering from leg injuries.

Immediately the investigation into the accident was begun and the priority was to identify the two unnamed victims. The lady with the letter was confirmed as being a wealthy young socialite, Emma Beaumont, who had been returning from a spell at Madame de Carnet's school on the Champs-Elysées. Emma's parents were both dead and she was possessed of a great personal fortune. One account suggested that she was returning to England to be married, but one would imagine that such a tragedy just days before a society wedding would dominate the news reports, so one may discount that supposition as the romantic imagination of a single journalist searching for a new angle on an already much-reported event. The other unidentified victim was the mysterious gentleman with HM darned into his socks. At Charing Cross Station only one set of luggage was not accounted for, that belonging to the French chef Hippolite Mercier. Monsieur Mercier's involvement in the tragedy was fully confirmed when his friend and fellow cook Leon Vanlangendouch, who was expecting a visit, became concerned.

Upon reading the news reports of the crash Mr Vanlangendouch contacted the South Eastern Railway company and the reality of the situation quickly became apparent. Instead of greeting his companion he was instead requested to formally identify the remains of the cook who had served Admiral Freemantle in Devonport.

There were some initial suspicions of two further bodies still under the wreckage but as the carriages were removed from the bed of the River Beult no remains were discovered and it was assumed that the official documentation as to who had travelled that day had been completed in error. Certainly, one gentleman in Paris had decided not to take the train that morning due to a severe attack of gout, the very condition that Charles Dickens had complained of before his trip to France.

On Sunday June 11th Dickens took the train from London to Higham (how must that journey have felt?) and at Gad's Hill Place he retired to his desk in the study where the letter writing resumed. The study at Gad's was at the front of the house and Charles's sloping desk was placed into the large bay window that bulged into the flowerbeds where scarlet geraniums, his favourite garden flower, were growing. The door to the study was lined with false book spines so when it was closed Charles appeared to be completely cocooned by literature, safe in his own world.

One of the first letters he wrote on that Sunday was to his estranged wife Catherine who, having read about the accident in the newspapers, had immediately written to inquire about her husband's wellbeing. Charles's letter of reply followed the pattern of those penned the day before; that is to say, he mentioned that he was in the only carriage not to go over the bridge, and that he spent two to three hours among the dead and the dying etc, but there was a certain sense of closeness and genuine friendship in his language, and he used the word 'affectionately' before scrawling his weak signature.

But Charles had also made a promise to Ellen and among the letters he wrote whilst at Gad's was one to the stationmaster at Charing Cross station:

GAD'S HILL PLACE, HIGHAM BY ROCHESTER, KENT.

Monday Twelfth June 1865

Dear Sir

A lady who was in the carriage with me in the terrible accident on Friday, lost, in the struggle of being got out of the carriage, a gold watch-chain with a smaller gold watch-chain attached, a bundle of charms, a gold watch-key, and a gold seal engraved 'Ellen'.

I promised the lady to make her loss known at headquarters, in case these trinkets should be found. Will you have the kindness to note this application.

The carriage was the first-class carriage which was dragged aslant, but did not go over, being caught upon the turn. The engine broke from it before, and the rest of the train broke from it behind and went down into the stream below.

I mention these particulars to make the lady's case plain.

I would have spoken to you instead of writing, but that I am shaken; — not by the beating of the carriage, but by the work afterwards of getting out the dying and dead.

Faithfully Yours CHARLES DICKENS

It was one the only letters he would write that mentioned Ellen by name, and for a man so anxious to wrap their relationship in mystery and so keen to keep her identity hidden it was an extraordinary oversight to be so open with a stranger. Whether or not the gold was ever found and returned we do not know and whether the stationmaster realised the importance of the document that lay on his desk is also uncertain, but the letter presumably was formally answered before being carefully filed away.

Dickens' health was a matter of great concern to him and in another letter to his friend John Forster he confided that 'I am curiously weak — weak as if I were recovering from a long illness. I begin to feel it more in my head. I sleep well and eat well; but I write half a dozen notes and turn faint and sick.'

Despite his concerns his letter writing at this time was prolific and on the same day that he had written to Forster he also wrote the long letter to Thomas Mitton which I have already quoted giving his own full account of the crash and averting to the two ladies who were his travelling companions: 'an old one and a young one', and which concluded with the admission 'that I don't want to be examined at the Inquest, and I don't want to write about it. It could do no good either way, and I could only seem to speak about myself, which, of course I would rather not do.'

Despite having written to the stationmaster and to Mitton, he knew that if he were interviewed the circumstances of his journey would be published in every newspaper and he didn't want to risk his carefully prepared and protected image of a good family man who shared wonderful Christmas feasts around a roaring fire becoming besmirched with scandal.

On the 17th June Charles wrote to Charles Fechter saying that 'I was in London yesterday, but had no idea you were at the theatre. I had promised to go up to Miss Coutts at Highgate, and I had to go to my doctor, and on other errands of business. The noise of the wheels of my Hansom, and of the London streets, was as much as I could bear. So I made all speed back here again — by a slow train, though, for I felt that I was not up to the Express.' This was written from Gad's Hill as were the letters he had dispatched on the 15th June, so he had travelled to London for a single day.

Presumably one of the 'other errands' he spoke of was to visit Ellen and spend time with her, maybe explaining to her what the stationmaster had told him about the lost collection of gold jewellery.

He certainly wanted her to be comfortable and on one occasion when he was back at Gad's Hill he wrote a short note to his manservant in London, John Thompson, asking him to 'take Miss Ellen tomorrow morning, a little basket of fresh fruit, a jar of clotted cream from Tuckers, and a chicken, a pair of pigeons, or some nice little bird. Also, on Wednesday morning, and on Friday morning, take her some other things of the same sort — making a little variety each day.'

Recovering a little from the shock Charles's journalistic ability soon returned and the letters began to display some of his old flair, even a touch of humour. For instance, to Mrs Lehman he wrote that 'I am quite right again, I thank God, and have even got my voice back; — I most unaccountably brought somebody else's out of that terrible scene.'

The subject matter of his correspondence became business-like again, discussing the continued publication of *Our Mutual Friend* with Wills and Forster, responding to the never-ending requests for patronages and appearances, sometimes enthusiastically if it were a cause in which he passionately believed, and sometimes using his experience and slow recovery as an excuse not to appear.

He also wrote to some of his fellow passengers. He had received a letter from Melville Merridew, the librarian from Boulogne, enquiring about his own health and recovery.

'I beg to thank you for your obliging enquiry,' wrote Dickens, 'and to assure you that I have not suffered any inconvenience from the terrible railway accident we encountered together, beyond an incapacity to bear much noise, and an occasional sense of weariness. I trust your shoulder will soon be better. I am not surprised by your taking time to find out that you were hurt, for I took to London in the carriage that conveyed me up from the scene of the disaster, two wounded passengers who have been lying ill ever since, and who had no notion at the time that there was much the matter with them.'

The writing of this reply prompted Dickens to seek out Mr Dickenson, the man he had rescued and travelled to London with and who was still recuperating at The Charing Cross Hospital.

Dear Sir

I send round my servant with this, to enquire how you are. I hope you will not suppose that I have been wanting in interest in you. On the very next morning after the accident, I spoke of you to the Station Master at Charing Cross, who (making some

144

mistake in the flurry of the time) did not couple you with my description. It was only on my going down to my country house last Friday, that he told me you were then still lying at the hotel.

Do not trouble yourself to try to write. If you could tell my servant by word of mouth how you are, I should be truly glad to know that you are doing well.

Faithfully Yours, CHARLES DICKENS

Edward Dickenson and Charles Dickens would continue to correspond and according to Mary Dickens, Charles's eldest daughter, Edward 'was a frequent visitor at Gad's Hill, and looked upon Charles Dickens as his preserver, the man to whom he owed his life'.

The Inquest

Day 1

In the modern era an inquiry into a disaster relies very much on electronic data collection and CCTV footage, all of which needs careful analysis before it can be submitted as evidence. In the nineteenth century, however, an inquest relied purely on the memories and observations of those immediately involved, so it was necessary to convene with as much expediency as possible. In the case of the Staplehurst crash the coroner for West Kent, Mr William Neve, opened the official hearing on the afternoon of Saturday 10 June, less than twenty-four hours after George Crombie had first sounded the whistle from his cab at the head of the tidal train. The hearing was held at the Railway Station Hotel in Staplehurst where upstairs Martin Condliff, Mr and Mrs Ralph and Major Francis still lay recovering in their beds.

The Staplehurst Railway Hotel today, ironically, seeing as he didn't attend the inquest, it is now named 'Dickens Court'

The jury of sixteen men was sworn in and their foreman was the Reverend Edward Moore from the nearby parish of Frittenden.

Mr Neve opened the hearing with a solemn address to the jurymen:

'Gentlemen, you are summoned here to inquire into the cause of the most lamentable event that has happened on the main line of the railway. You are now to inquire into the death of ten persons, who were passengers in the tidal train yesterday afternoon on this line, which ran off the line at a place not far from here, and which portion of the line was at that time under repair.

'In the exercise of your duty you will have to inquire who has been to blame — whether he was executing those repairs on the approach of a train at an improper time, whether the signalman was guilty of any breach of duty in not signalling proper notice, or whether the driver of the train was guilty of any gross negligence in disregarding those signals.

'But today we had better confine ourselves to identifying the bodies of the unfortunate deceased, and to the medical evidence as to the immediate cause of death, then adjourn to some day next week, which will be convenient to all parties, when the great question can be gone into.'

The coroner and the jury as well as representatives of the South Eastern Railway Company and witnesses then boarded a train which took them just a mile along the track to the scene of the crash so that they could see the state of the rails for themselves and from there back to a shed where nine of the ten bodies lay and here the awful business of identification began.

Lloyd Rayner, the merchant from Liverpool, identified

body number 8 as that of his wife Amelia. He confirmed that she was thirty-seven years old and she had been travelling back to Liverpool from Paris. He had received a letter from her written on the day before the accident confirming that she would be on the tidal train that day. Besides Lloyd junior, who lay in Staplehurst Place with his broken arm, the heartbroken husband also told the jury that Amelia left five other children.

Body number 7 was identified by Frederick Bodenham as being his wife Annie and he described the circumstances of her death: he and Annie had been in one of the central first- class carriages and he had heard her voice at the moment that the carriage had fallen from the bridge. He had been thrown from the carriage into the water but remarkably was uninjured and when he came to his senses found his new wife trapped in the remains of their compartment four or five minutes later. She was dead and her body was carefully removed and laid on the riverbank.

In answer to a question from the Reverend Moore, Bodenham was certain that the train's brakes had not been applied prior to the crash and that they had been travelling at an unabated speed as they reached the breach in the line, a claim that would be discounted by the bulk of evidence that was to come.

John Lomax, an auctioneer from Bolton formally confirmed the identification of the surgeon Adam Hampson, body number 9. (His widow Elizabeth was recovering in London and was therefore not called upon to appear.) Mr Lomax went on to explain that he was a close friend to Mr Hampson and that he had known that the couple were travelling from Paris back to London on the 9th June.

George Whitby sorrowfully identified body number 3 as

that of his wife Lydia who was 28 years old. They lived together in St James' Street in London and he had been expecting her home the previous evening.

Body number 4 was that of Caroline White, a fact confirmed by the Reverend Arthur Thompson of Portman Square, London. He had been a friend of hers for many years and described her as 'a traveller'. She had resided in a particularly elegant and respectable neighbourhood of Brighton and in recent years had wintered in the equally fashionable French town of Pau. She was 53.

John Hill Elder, a solicitor who resided at 333 City Road, Islington confirmed that James Dunn of the same address was the identity of body number 2. James Dunn was a warehouseman and had been due to disembark from the tidal train in London and catch the quarter past nine train to Dundee. Dunn was a single man and had been travelling alone.

David Ovenden of the Kent Police was then called upon to give evidence regarding the identity of the other bodies. He explained that body number 1 was that of the, as yet unidentified, male with 'HM' darned into his socks (even as the evidence was being heard in Staplehurst Leon Vanlangendouch was making enquiries at Charing Cross station and discovering that his friend and fellow chef Hippolite Mercier was dead), and that body number 5 was that of the beautiful, and rich, young woman Emma Beaumont.

Body number 6 was a woman whose linen was marked 'Condliff'. She appeared well dressed and 'apparently in good circumstances'. Mr Ovenden supposed that this was the wife of Martin Condliff who was lying injured in the same building and tragically, it was reported 'in moments of delirious wanderings fondly imagines she still lives'.

Only one victim was left to be formally identified and the coroner ordered that the court should make its way to Chapman Farmhouse, on Pristling Lane in Staplehurst which was owned by a local landowner John Reeves. It was here that Mrs Charlotte Faithfull lay and was identified by her husband, the judge who had returned from Bombay. Hers was body number 10.

Doctor Wilkins, the Staplehurst surgeon, was called and he was asked to confirm that all the deaths were as a result of injuries consistent with the violence of the accident, which he did.

At 7:30 pm Mr Neve adjourned proceedings and called for the inquest to resume on Monday June 12th at 2:30 pm.

Day 2

When coroner and jury assembled again, they were joined by a large gathering of imposing professional gentlemen. Mr Eborall and Mr Knight from the South Eastern Railway Company journeyed back to Kent once more, having returned to London on the last of the relief trains just two days before. The company's legal interests were in the hands of their solicitor Mr Freeland and his team, whilst for technical evidence Mr James Cudworth, the Superintendent of the Locomotive Department (who had been responsible for the design of the locomotive that had been at the head of the train), was present.

Almost all of the victims, as well as many of the injured, were represented by their own solicitors, meaning that The Station Hotel was rather overcrowded as Mr Neve called for order and requested that David Ovenden, the Superintendent of the Kent Police, bring Henry Benge into the 'court'; he was represented by a local solicitor from Cranbrook, John Minter. Also present throughout the inquest was Captain Rich of the Royal Engineers who had been appointed to write the official Board of Trade report into the circumstances of the disaster.

The first witness to be called was Edward Coleman, a carpenter who had been working on the refurbishment of the three bridges over the Beult.

Coleman confirmed that he had been working for the railway company for nearly three years and had been engaged on the River Beult job since its start. He gave an accurate account of the work that was being carried out and explained exactly how the rails were lifted, the timbers removed and replaced. He confirmed that the rails had been re-laid so that the earlier train could pass without incident. He explained how John Wiles had been sent up the line with the red flag but he did not know if any fog signals had been laid (they had not been). Initially he did not hear the train approach but was alerted to the fact by another member of the team, then he heard the whistle '…when the train was nearer to me than the signalman was. It was a continuous whistle at first. The train did not appear to slacken, as it came on very fast indeed; but you could not tell in the confusion. We ran towards the train when we first heard the whistle, making all the signs we could to stop the train.'

The questioning then moved onto the character of Henry Benge himself and the circumstances of the timetable:

'Did you hear him say anything about the boat train being due that afternoon?'

'I heard him say — at breakfast time, I think — that it was due at 5:20. He was then looking at the general service time-book. John Dawson had another book, but it was no use, having been partially destroyed. Benge can read moderately well. I have several times heard him reading his Bible at dinner and other mealtimes.'

Edward Coleman was thanked, and he stood down having given a clear, comprehensive and unemotional account of the day.

Next to be called was one of the platelayers, William Allen, who stated that the crew had worked from 6:00 am until breakfast time, when, although he had sat next to Mr Coleman, he was NOT aware of Henry Benge studying the timetable book at that time. He had also been employed by the company for three years and knew Benge well, and thought him to be a 'steady man'.

Following the passing of the 2:50 up train the rails had been removed once more and work continued. The job they were undertaking would normally take about an hour and a quarter, although some timbers came out more easily than others.

In reply to a question about the speed of the train posed by Captain Usborne, one of the jurors, Mr Allen stated that it came on at the normal speed of a tidal train, that he had first seen it when it was about a mile away and assumed it would stop but it kept 'coming at such a stroke'.

It is interesting to point out that three of the witnesses interviewed so far had all testified that the train had not braked at all and that it arrived at the bridge at undiminished speed, but the technical evidence given by James Cudworth and Mr Healey, an engineer from Darlington, clearly stated that the brakes of the locomotive and those in the surviving carriages were applied and that the levers in the cab proved that George Crombie had reversed the drive to assist in the rapid retardation.

Lawrence Mercer, who had been one of the guards on the train, was called and for the first time the jury heard an account from the train itself. Mercer stated that he had worked as a guard on the South Eastern Line for thirteen years, he knew George Crombie the driver well and felt him to be a very careful, steady man.

On the afternoon of June 9th, the train had met the steamer at Folkestone. Most of the passengers travelling to London, around 100, although he was not certain as to the exact number, had made the crossing from France. The tidal train had departed at half past two. The service was due to run through all the stations on the route until it reached Redhill and it passed Headcorn station at eleven or twelve minutes past three.

'My attention was first called to danger by the danger signal given by the driver. The danger signal which the driver gave was two whistles, closely following each other. I saw no danger flag, nor did I look for one, but I applied the brake as soon as I heard the whistle. I applied three brakes, the one I spoke of and the two patent brakes attached to a first-class carriage on the train. I cannot say what distance it was after I put on the brake before the accident occurred. It might have been half a mile, but I cannot speak positively. I succeeded in slackening the speed considerably. We had been travelling that time at 45 or 50 miles per hour. I applied all the brake power I could. We had reduced the speed perhaps to 15 miles per hour when the train ran off the line.'

The evidence of Mr Mercer is very much at odds with that of Frederick Bodenham, who stated that the train went over the bridge at unabated speed, rather than the frantic hard braking that the guard described. With the severity of the wreckage it is inconceivable that the speed at the time of the accident was as low as 15 miles be hour and the truth of the situation was inevitably somewhere between the two.

The questioning then moved onto the issue of the warning flag:

'At Headcorn station the "all right" signal was exhibited. The distance at which we can see a signal-flag on the line depends on the atmosphere. A bright sun will often prevent a signal-flag from being seen. There was a brilliant sun at that time. Sometimes the steam blowing will prevent our seeing the signals. I was not at all aware of the repairs going on on the bridge.'

The Reverend Moore pursued this line of questioning and Mercer continued his evidence:

'We are expected to keep a general lookout, but not so much at places like that where the accident occurred as when we are passing or near stations. The longest distance, I should think, at which I could see a red flag signal would be half a mile, but I could not say for certain.'

One important fact to remember in regard of this evidence is that Lawrence Mercer was in a guard's van behind the locomotive and the tender, meaning that any view of the line that he had would have been seriously obscured. Another juryman pressed him on this point:

'The engine driver is always on the lookout. The remark about the difficulty in seeing the danger flag in sunlight does not apply to the driver as it does to the guard. The driver will necessarily have to take his eyes from looking ahead for ten seconds.

'I saw the flag after the accident. The man appeared to be

holding it in his hand behind the train. I cannot say how far behind, but I should say about 150 yards. I cannot say whether the man had moved or not.'

After more questions had been asked about the braking systems and the method of communications between the driver and the guards, the coroner asked the prisoner, Henry Benge, if he had any questions he would like to put to the witness. The poor man said that he did not and rather sorrowfully mumbled that the train was much further from the bridge when the notice of danger was given than Mercer had stated.

The inquest was adjourned once more and Mr Neve declared that it would sit again on Friday 16th June, exactly a week after the crash.

Day 3

The third day of the hearing would see the cross-examination of three star witnesses: George Crombie and William Beattie (the driver and fireman of the tidal train respectively) would give their evidence from the view of the footplate and Mr Joseph Gallimore, the inspector of the permanent way would also be questioned about his supervisory position. As befitted such an important day the venue of the inquest was changed from the small Station Hotel to a much larger room at the Torrington Hotel nearby.

Mr Ovenden once again brought Henry Benge into the room and one journalist remarked that he appeared to be a 'harmless, inoffensive looking man'. He was now represented by a new solicitor, Mr Ody from London.

The first witness to be called was Peter Ashcroft, the Chief Engineer for the South Eastern Railway Company, a role that he had held for eleven years. Mr Ashcroft confirmed that the repairs on the stretch of line across the fields to the south of Staplehurst were being carried out under the inspection of Mr Gallimore, who was responsible for the section of track between Ashford and Tonbridge, and that he (Mr Ashcroft), had no knowledge of them.

In a remarkable piece of corporate buck-passing Ashcroft then stated that 'it was Mr Gallimore's duty to see to the safety of the line under his contract, and it was also his duty to report any irregularity. But in this instance, none, I apprehend, has arisen because that which was to be done could be done without diverting the trains. Mr Gallimore would deal with any irregularities of the platelayers himself.'

The coroner, the foreman of the jury and other jury members then asked Mr Ashcroft a series of questions and almost every answer he gave began with 'Mr Gallimore....' leaving all present in no doubt as to where the blame really lay.

In an unfortunate quirk of scheduling the next witness to be called was Joseph Gallimore himself.

Using the technique that had proved so successful for his superior Gallimore told the jury that he had appointed Henry Benge as a foreman of platelayers, that Benge had made the usual declaration required of any man appointed to a position of responsibility, that he had warned Benge to be very careful to not break a line up when there was any danger of a train coming. Gallimore confirmed that Benge had been given a book of rules but had not actually asked if he had read it.

As far as the current works on the line were concerned Joseph confirmed that he had ordered that they be carried out and that the work was taking much longer than he had estimated as the timbers were in a much worse state than anyone had realised. It was Henry Benge's responsibility to continually check his stretch of line, making sure that the metal keys were tight, and that the permanent way was secure. Benge was required to write a weekly report outlining any specific problems and Gallimore produced a copy of a recent one for the jury to see. 'The signature is his, but not the body of the report. I have seen him write his name, nothing more.'

At no stage did Mr Ody, Henry Benge's solicitor, ask a question or challenge a statement and the prisoner, the only man to have been committed to custody, listened in the knowledge that he had become the scapegoat for the entire incident and that the responsibility for ten deaths lay entirely on his broad shoulders. The sad thing is that he probably believed it to be true.

The day's evidence continued, and the driver George Crombie was called. His evidence didn't add much to that already heard, for it was remarkably similar to that given by Lawrence Mercer the guard: the train had been running at 40 — 50 miles per hour, and the bright sun may have prevented him from noticing the signalman any earlier. He had whistled to the fireman and the guards so that they could apply the brakes, and then shut off steam and reversed the engine. He could have done no more. He admitted that three quarters of a mile was a long distance to bring the train to a halt but countered that with the observation that fifty miles an hour was a great speed.

Under cross-examination Crombie definitely stated that John Wiles had been positioned only a matter of 150 yards from the viaduct and certainly not 500, not even 400. This figure was exactly the same as that given by Mercer and suggests a great deal of conversation had taken place between them, so that blame might be shifted away from those on board the train and towards the labourers.

Whatever story had been hatched out between Crombie, Mercer and William Beattie (the fireman on the train whose evidence firmly backed up that of the other two), their collective estimate as to the position of John Wiles was disproved by the evidence of two labourers who had been working in the fields near to Sloman's Crossing and had noticed him waving the flag as the train approached. This distance had been formally measured as part of the proceedings and was entered into the evidence as 544 yards.

The final witness to be called was Cornelius Eborall, the director of the rail company, who established that the rules regarding safety on the line were firmly set and that they were issued to all men involved in such work and that it was the responsibility of the foreman to ensure that everyone was aware of those regulations.

An accident of this nature had never occurred on the tidal train. Indeed, no person had ever been injured on the tidal train before and the South Eastern Railway Company was proud of its record. In a display of solidarity for his workers he pointed out that nowhere in the evidence given had it been suggested that Henry Benge, or any of the crew, were not intelligent men: 'these men are not uneducated men. They are not highly educated, but they are men of intelligence, of education, and of nerve, and they would more efficiently discharge their duties than educated men.' Of Benge specifically Mr Eborall said, 'He is a very steady man, and I am sorry to see him in such a position, as I consider him to be a very good man.'

And so the coroner brought the case to a close. He summed up and told the jury that they must find their verdict purely based on the evidence they had heard. It had been proved, he said, that the ten people who had lost their lives had done so as a result of injuries sustained when the train ran off the bridge. The accident had occurred because a stretch of rail had been lifted. It was certain the Henry Benge was in charge of the works and had ordered that the work commence at 2:51, only 28 minutes before the tidal train was due. Benge had admitted to Mr Ovenden and to Mr Eborall in evidence that he had read the timetable incorrectly and that he wasn't expecting the tidal train for another two hours, by which time the work would have been completed.

As to Joseph Gallimore Mr Neve pointed out that he had the responsibility for the overall supervision of the works and should have ensured that every safety precaution was taken, for example that the correct number of fog signals should have been placed, and that the distance that John Wiles had been sent to display the red flag should have been properly considered.

George Crombie, the driver, he exonerated completely and said that he had taken all of the actions that he could to stop the train, but it was a sad fact that there was not enough distance available to him and that the crash was therefore inevitable.

And with that Mr Neve, the coroner for the West Kent district instructed the jury to retire and to consider their verdict. It was twenty minutes to five on Friday 16 June.

After two hours of deliberation the jury returned. The Reverend Moore stood and said, 'Our verdict is one of Manslaughter against Joseph Gallimore and Henry Benge.'

Mr Neve asked how many of the jury agreed with the verdict and was told 'twelve against Joseph Gallimore and sixteen against Henry Benge. I am desired by the majority of the jury to append this to our verdict: "The jury fully recognising the general sufficiency of the company's rules to ensure the public safety, yet strongly recommend that when possible notice should be given from the previous station of any works involving the breaking of the line.'"

Mr Eborall then stood to make a statement on behalf of the company: 'Mr Coroner, and gentlemen of the jury, I will take care that the recommendation is placed before the directors of the South Eastern Railway Company, and I am quite sure they will give it their most serious consideration. Before leaving here today I have to express my regret on behalf of the company that you should have been called to inquire into so serious a calamity, and I trust that means will be taken to prevent another such occurrence. I also have publicly to thank you all residents in this neighbourhood for the kind, humane and Christian attention paid to the unfortunate sufferers by this dreadful calamity.' At the conclusion of this statement the members of the jury cheered and clapped in honour of the residents of Staplehurst.

The only formal duty remaining was for the Coroner to draw up warrants for committal of Mr Joseph Gallimore and Mr Henry Benge, both of whom were led away by David Ovenden.

When the deaths of the ten victims were entered into the official records each bore the same words in the Cause of Death column: 'Feloniously killed by Joseph Gallimore and Henry Benge'.

That Charles Dickens did not appear at the inquest was no great surprise, for none of the other passengers was called to give evidence either, with the exception of those who had appeared on the first day to identify their loved ones.

The Board of Trade Report

On 22 June 1865 a letter was sent from the Board of Trade (Railway Department) to Mr James Booth, the Secretary of the South Eastern Railway Company:

'Sir —

I am directed by the Lords of the Committee of the Privy Council for Trade to transmit to you, to be laid before the Directors of the South Eastern Railway Company the enclosed copy of the report made by Captain Rich RE, the officer appointed by their Lordships to inquire into the circumstances connected with the accident which occurred on the 9th instant, to the tidal passenger train near Staplehurst on the South Eastern Railway.

'My Lords trust that the directors will give the recommendations contained in Captain Rich's report their careful consideration.'

Attached to the letter was the official report which Captain Rich had compiled, based on the evidence he had heard throughout the inquest at Staplehurst in the immediate aftermath of the crash.

The report began by explaining the nature of the repairs and then that the foreman of the platelayers, Henry Benge (although he was referred to as John Benge throughout the document), had incorrectly read the timetable at breakfast and had expected the train to arrive two hours later than it was due.

'Notwithstanding the mistake of the foreman as to the time of arrival of the tidal train, no accident would have happened, had the regulations existing on the South Eastern Railway been adhered to.'

Firstly, Captain Rich chose to point out the requirement to place fog signals along the route if the line was being taken up. 'This regulation was disregarded on the 9th June, and was not properly carried out by the foreman of the platelayers in charge of the length of line between Headcorn and Staplehurst stations, during any part of the ten weeks that the work had been going on.'

The Captain then moved onto the length of time over which the work had been carried out: 'It is also the custom and rule on the South Eastern Railway when "protracted repairs" are executed that the engineer should report them to the manager, so that the latter gentleman may issue printed notices of the repairs and their locality to all persons concerned. Such printed notices are referred to in the printed monthly service timetables.

'This precaution, a most necessary one to insure drivers looking out when approaching parts of the road under repair, was also omitted in the present case.

'The engineer states that the work on the viaducts was not looked upon as a "protracted repair" because each baulk or separate portion of the whole could be taken out, renewed and the road made perfect, in the intervals between trains passing. I cannot agree in this view and consider that a repair that requires the breaking of the permanent way (sometimes three times a day) at intervals for a period of ten weeks, or even for a much shorter period, should be looked upon as a "protracted repair".'

What Captain Rich did not point out was that during the ten weeks preceding the accident the team had worked quite safely and effectively and had repaired the permanent way before any trains were due. Indeed, they had done so earlier on the afternoon of the 9th June. However, if the case had been listed as a protracted repair the main difference would have been that George Crombie, the driver of the train, would have had prior knowledge of the repairs and could have proceeded with more caution instead of letting the locomotive have its head.

The report went on to describe the scene of the crash and the works that led to it in greater detail, calling on the evidence that had been given at the inquest. Generally, Captain Rich simply laid out facts, but occasionally in the report he would offer his own opinions, for example when dealing with the issue of the speed at which the train had been travelling:

'The driver... states that he had reduced his speed from 45 or 50 miles per hour to ten miles per hour (the figure agreed upon by the driver, fireman and guard and included in each of their testimonies). I consider that his estimate of the speed to which he reduced his train is erroneous; and considering the time that would be lost before the brakes came into action, and the result of the catastrophe, it appears probable that he had not reduced the speed of the train below 30 miles per hour when he reached the viaduct.'

In his words Captain Rich attached no blame to George Crombie, but certainly gave him an official rap over the knuckles for trying to reinvent the facts.

Having presented all of the circumstances of the case: the braking capability of the train, the positioning of John Wiles, the length of the breach, the positions of the various carriages after the crash, etc, Captain Rich presented his conclusion:

'Before concluding this report, I think it right to call attention to the circumstances that this melancholy disaster has occurred on a perfectly straight and nearly level part of the South Eastern Railway where the permanent way is kept in excellent order. It has happened to a train which had a good proportion of brake power, was drawn by a first-class engine and made up in a proper manner with communication between guards and driver.

'In all human possibility this train would have reached London safely (even though the route was broken at the Beult Viaduct) had the rules of the South Eastern Company been adhered to. The provisions in these rules for always using fog signals when rails are taken up is an additional precaution not generally adopted by railway companies.

'It appears, however, for the last ten weeks these rules have been daily disregarded on the line between Headcorn and Staplehurst, and that the inspector of the permanent way who is supposed to visit every part of the line several times during the week, if he is unable to do so daily, took no notice of such disobedience of the rules, though it does not appear possible for him to be ignorant of the fact.

'I fear that the regulations which provide for signalmen going out certain distances, and guards going back with flags, to protect disabled trains, which are in existence on railways generally, are too often disregarded and only partially carried out.

'It appears also improper that a work of such extent as the renewal of the longitudinal timbers on several viaducts, occupying a period of ten weeks, should be carried on without the knowledge of the engineer of the railway, and consequently without any notice to the drivers and others employed on the line.

'I would suggest, for the future, that the inspectors be called upon to furnish returns weekly, or at such stated intervals as may appear best, showing the works in progress, and the date of their visits to those works, which can be easily checked by corresponding entries by the station masters or other officials. It might also be useful for them to state that they have satisfied themselves that the men under them understand and carry out their orders.

'If these returns include all of the events that may occur in their district, they will afford the engineer and all other officers of the Company the means of checking, for the future, such irregularities as have caused this fearful calamity.

'The result of the coroner's inquest is a verdict of manslaughter against the foreman of the platelayers and the district inspector of the permanent way.

I have &c

FH Rich. Capt. RE.'

The Board of Trade report was purely intended to suggest improvements to the policies so that such tragedies could be avoided in the future, and Captain Rich certainly laid out what he felt should be changed from an administrative point of view, but it seems remarkable that he did not mention the request from the inquest jury that in the case of an interruption to the line a signal of warning should have been shown at the previous station. In the case of Staplehurst a number of witnesses testified that the signals at Headcorn station were set

165

to 'all clear' and the guard Lawrence Mercer stated that, 'We are expected to keep a general lookout, but not so much at places like that where the accident occurred as when we are passing or near stations.'

If the signals at Headcorn had been set to 'danger' at 11 minutes past 3 on the 9th June 1865, it wouldn't have mattered that the train arrived two hours before it was expected, it wouldn't have mattered that John Wiles was standing 544 yards from the bridge, instead of 1,000 with his flag, it wouldn't have mattered that there were no fog signals placed, it wouldn't have mattered that the driver was looking into a bright sun on a dead straight stretch of line. All that would have happened was that George Crombie would have reacted to the signal, shut off steam and brought the speed of the train down to a crawling pace. For the simple expedient of a signal being shown at a spot where a driver would naturally be looking for it ten lives would have been saved and the demons of death and disaster would not continue to torment the survivors.

The Kentish Assizes

The final act of the Staplehurst rail crash tragedy was played out at The Maidstone Crown Court at the summer sitting of the Kentish Assizes which commenced on Tuesday 25th July.

The case against Joseph Gallimore and Henry Benge would be heard by the Judge Mr Baron Piggot who arrived with great pomp on Monday 24th. According to *The Dover Telegraph* he 'arrived at Maidstone shortly after two o'clock by the North Kent Railway. He was received at the station by the High Sheriff (R. Rodger Esq), F. Sendimore Esq (Under Sheriff), and the Sheriff's Chaplain the Reverend James Moneypenny, by whom he was escorted to his lodgings, where he was waited on by the Mayor and corporation wearing their robes of office. His Lordship at three o'clock proceeded to the Church of All Saints where an impressive sermon was preached by the Chaplain. After service the learned Judge proceeded to the court, where the commission was opened in due course, and the Court adjourned till Tuesday.'

Charles Dickens himself would have delighted in writing such a scene of splendid pomposity peopled with a cast of grotesques.

There was such a full list of cases to be heard when the court reconvened on Tuesday, meaning that Gallimore and Benge would have to wait to be called. The first was against

John Smith, Henry Thompson (alias John Palsford) and James Smith (alias James Bruton) who were severally accused of 'setting fire to a stack of bean straw at Folkestone on 12th June'. All of the arsonists were found guilty and sentenced to seven years penal servitude.

The next was another of arson, this time in Sittingbourne. William Johnson was found guilty of setting fire to a stack of wheat valued at £220 and was given the same sentence.

'Robbing a Fellow Lodger at Sheerness' was next up. Thomas Green, a 20-year-old marine, was accused of stealing a watch and other articles belonging to Leonard Sibell. Once again, the defendant was found guilty and he was sentenced to twelve months hard labour.

Two tragic cases were then heard, both involving the death of children, which give us a real sense of the horror of poverty in the 1860s. Firstly, Ellen Mitchell was accused of the manslaughter of her child Sophia. Ellen was taken to the Medway Union Workhouse during February 1861 where, in a scene reminiscent of the opening chapters of *Oliver Twist*, she gave birth to a little girl. In May of the same year she left the workhouse, taking the child with her who at that time was in good health. In July little Sophia was returned to the establishment in a terribly emaciated state, and despite the best endeavours to save her she died there in September.

Evidence was offered that the child died by 'want of proper nourishment', but the defence vehemently argued that the death of Sophia may have been caused by disease, and pleaded their client's innocence, stating that she had been unable to procure a living but had divided her meagre means with her child; the protestations were rejected and Ellen Mitchell, aged 33, was sentenced to twelve months hard labour.

The final case to be tried on Tuesday bore the awful title of 'Concealment of Birth'. Emma Robinson, a 25-year-old servant, was indicted for secretly disposing of the dead body of her baby by throwing it down a privy in the village of North Cray, near Bexley. She was sentenced to six months hard labour.

For all that Charles Dickens would have relished the pomposity and comic opportunities of the arrival of Baron Pigott on Monday, he would also have embraced the awful tragedy of the two children's deaths and done whatever he could to improve the lot of others in the same plight and to raise awareness in the court of public opinion.

On Wednesday two cases (one of counterfeiting and one of housebreaking) were heard before Henry Benge and Joseph Gallimore were called to answer their charges of manslaughter of diverse passengers on the tidal train, but specifically for the death of Hannah Condliff. Benge had yet another solicitor to argue his case (the third since the start of the inquest), this time Mr Ribton.

The evidence heard was the same as had been presented at the inquest and many of the same witnesses were called, but Ribton argued his client's case much more forcibly than either Mr Ody or Mr Minter had previously. When he rose to make his closing remarks, he gave a 'most able address'. He argued that whilst he could not deny that the railway company had done everything in their power to prevent such an accident occurring by putting firm rules in place, it was nonetheless clear that if the signalman had done his duty and made his way to the 1,000 yards mark, and if the engine driver had kept a proper lookout, the accident could have been prevented. It was unquestionable, continued Mr Ribton warming to his theme, that the prisoner had grounds for complaining that he alone had been singled out as a scapegoat when the previously named individuals appeared to be quite as much involved. Laying down these arguments he pointed out to the jury that it would be 'very unjust to make him alone responsible'.

With Mr Ribton's closing remarks hanging in the air it was then time for the Judge to sum up the case. In *The Pickwick Papers* Charles Dickens described the way in which Justice Stareleigh summed up in the great trial of Bardell vs Pickwick and had the novel not been written 29 years previously it might have been supposed that the author took inspiration from Baron Piggot. In *Pickwick*, Dickens had written:

'He read as much of his notes to the jury as he could decipher on so short a notice; he didn't read as much of them as he couldn't make out and made running— comments on the evidence as he went along. If Mrs Bardell were right, it was perfectly clear that Mr Pickwick was wrong, and if they thought the evidence of Mrs Cluppins worthy of credence, they would believe it, and, if they didn't, why, they wouldn't.'

In the reality of Maidstone Crown Court Mr Piggot pointed out that the prisoner had been charged with causing the death of Hannah Condliff by negligence and the first question was, how was the death occasioned? She was a traveller in an express train at the rate of fifty miles an hour, and the train came to a spot where a portion of rails had been removed, and there were no rails to go upon, and the consequence was that the train was thrown off the line and the deceased thereby met her death, and the jury would have to say who was responsible.

'The learned counsel for the prisoner has endeavoured to argue that other persons had contributed to the event, but he could not at all subscribe to such a doctrine, and, if it were allowed to prevail, in a case like the present, if the signalman was accused he would say it was not his fault but the fault of the person who had caused the rail to be removed, and each would throw the blame upon the other. The real question was, who was responsible for the act which was, undoubtedly, the cause of the calamity.'

The Judge was firmly steering the jury towards the suggestion that Henry Benge, the foreman of the platelayers, was wholly responsible for the Staplehurst rail crash. Sure enough, when the jury returned from their deliberations, they acquitted Joseph Gallimore and duly found Henry Benge guilty.

Passing sentence on Benge Mr Baron Pigott said: 'You have been found guilty of culpable negligence in the performance of your duty, which resulted in the death of the unhappy lady Hannah Condliff. The jury have expressed an opinion, with which I very much agree that such a duty as yours — namely, that being in command over a body of men employed in taking up the iron rails, on a line over which express trains are constantly travelling, aught not to be intrusted to a mere ordinary labourer who works with his pickaxe and shovel at the same employment. I hope the railway company will take this into their serious consideration. Giving due weight to this opinion of the jury, and also to the fact that you have received an excellent character for sobriety and steadiness, I think that the sentence of nine months' imprisonment which I now pass upon you will be sufficient.'

With that all formal proceedings relating to the great disaster at Staplehurst were concluded.

PART THREE:
LIFE AFTER STAPLEHURST

What Happened Next?

Once the various enquiries, inquests and court cases had been completed the story of Staplehurst faded from the newspapers as more current stories filled the columns, but for those immediately involved their lives and memories would be haunted by the events that had taken place on the 9th June 1865.

Lloyd Rayner, the Liverpool merchant, had travelled to Staplehurst where he identified the body of his wife Amelia and when the formalities had been completed, and having been assured that his son Lloyd junior was sufficiently recovered to make a journey he returned to the family home in Toxteth where he and his six children tried to come to terms with the fact that they would never see Amelia again. Amelia was buried in St James' Cemetery in Liverpool.

Lloyd remarried in 1868 and continued to ply his successful trade importing and exporting goods from the docks on the banks of the River Mersey up until the time of his death in January 1876.

The Liverpool Daily Post reported, 'The funeral of Lloyd Rayner, whose death we recorded last week took place on Saturday at the Smithdown Road cemetery and was attended by a large concourse of gentlemen in business by whom the deceased was highly respected, and who came to pay the last token of regard to a gentleman whom they had long held in the most profound esteem.' Elsewhere in that same edition was a report of 'A Serious Railway Collision'. At Tamworth station a mail train was hit from behind by a coal train on the same line. Eleven years on from Staplehurst and there were still serious issues regarding signalling on the rail network in Britain.

In the same cemetery where Lloyd Rayner had been laid to rest was the grave of Hannah Condliff who had been interred on the 15th June eleven years previously. Hannah and her husband Martin had owned and managed a coastal hotel in the small town of Waterloo near Crosby and when he had fully recovered from his injuries Martin returned to the North-west where he advertised that 'The Queen's Hotel. Having undergone extensive alterations is now replete with every comfort for the Accommodation of Visitors and Private Families.'

Martin, you will recall, had lain injured in The Staplehurst Railway Hotel while the inquest took place in the rooms below. In moments of delirium he suffered terrible delusions that his wife Hannah was still alive. He was a difficult patient but gradually he was nursed to health. He remarried and his new bride was Catherine Lord, a teacher, sister to Mary Ann Lord, the Staplehurst schoolmistress, who together had cared for him in the days after the crash. The wedding took place in Kent less than a year after the accident and in time the Lord family would move from Staplehurst to Liverpool where they would all live in The Queen's Hotel where they were listed in the 1871 Census.

Martin died in Liverpool in 1885, aged 56 years old.

Frederick Bodenham returned to Hereford where he buried his young wife Annie in the City Cemetery. They had enjoyed their last days together travelling in France and relishing all that Paris had to offer. The last words she had spoken to him were as the train went over the bridge and she cried out for help.

Frederick was a successful solicitor and for his whole life worked as a partner in the company originally formed by his uncles and cousin: James and Bodenham. Throughout his life Frederick had a keen interest in politics and was a prominent and active member of the local Liberal party. He was appointed to the position of Clerk of the Peace and later was unanimously elected as a Town Councillor and campaigned vigorously for the interests of the city of Hereford.

Frederick Bodenham

He married again, and with his new wife Laura had two daughters, Kathaleen and Laura, born in 1869 and 1870, respectively. It is more than likely that Frederick and Laura went to watch Charles Dickens as he performed in the Shire Hall in Hereford on April 11th, 1867. One of the pieces that Charles performed that evening was The Trial from *Pickwick* and no doubt Frederick enjoyed the merciless lampooning of the legal industry. However, there is no record that the two men, whose lives had touched so briefly in 1865, actually met.

Frederick Bodenham died in 1891 from a huge stroke. He was only 57 years old. Although *The Hereford Gazette* described the funeral as being 'of a private nature', the list of attendees was long and impressive, all paying their last respects to a popular gentleman who had certainly left his mark on the world.

Edward Dickenson, the young man that Charles had helped from the wreckage, joined the army, his regiment being the Lancashire Fusiliers, and was promoted to the rank of captain and later major.

As I have previously mentioned Edward became a regular visitor at Gad's Hill Place and even spent the Christmas of 1865 as a guest of the Dickens family. In a letter to John Forster a few weeks after the crash Charles confirmed that 'the railway people have offered, in the case of the young man whom I got out of the carriage just alive all the expenses and a thousand pounds down'. And it was only through Charles's influence that Edward was not sent to join his regiment in India.

Others also received compensation from the South Eastern Railway company and in December it was reported that Charles Landour, one of the French passengers on the tidal train, had been awarded £1,500 in damages, although he had needed to fight for it in the courts.

Henry Benge, the foreman of platelayers, who had been found solely culpable of the deaths at Staplehurst served six months of his nine month sentence. Unsurprisingly he did not return to employment with the South Eastern Railway Company but toiled in the fields of Kent as an agricultural labourer. He was mentally tormented by his involvement in the crash and was eventually admitted into the Kent County Lunatic Hospital in Maidstone. Henry Benge died in the asylum in May 1905 almost exactly forty years after the disaster. He was buried in the village of Sutton Valance, just five miles from Staplehurst.

And how about the most celebrated passenger on the train, and his companions, what did the future hold for Charles Dickens and Ellen Ternan?

It was apparent that Charles and Ellen were returning to England in order to start a new life together, although Victorian morals and sense of propriety meant that they would never be able to actually live together beneath the same roof. Charles was safely ensconced at Gad's Hill Place, his country house in Kent, whilst the only home that Ellen had was her mother's in Ampthill Square near Euston station in London, but soon she would be living in a cottage in Slough, undoubtedly paid for and maintained by Charles Dickens himself.

Slough was in a perfect situation for Charles and Ellen, as it was outside the bustle of the city (and all of the attention that that brought), but it was close to three mainline railway stations, meaning that Charles could travel with ease from or to the terminuses at Paddington, Waterloo or Victoria, meaning there was never a strict pattern or routine. Charles went to huge lengths to keep the relationship quiet and following the indiscretions in his correspondence after the accident he made every attempt to keep Ellen hidden from the prying eyes of the press and public.

As far as the rent book was concerned the house was kept by Mr Tringham (initially 'John', but later 'Charles') and although some locals knew full well that Mr Tringham was in fact Mr Dickens, the residents of the small town maintained a respectful silence, as those in the little town of Condette near Boulogne, where Charles and Ellen kept their 'love nest', did also.

Although the train network was a central part of his secret life Charles Dickens was now a nervous and at times terrified passenger. Towards the end of June 1865, he wrote to John Forster stating that 'I cannot bear railway travelling yet. A perfect conviction, against the senses, that the carriage is down on one side (and generally that is the left, and not the side on which the carriage in the accident really went over) comes upon me with anything like speed, and is inexpressibly distressing.' A few weeks after that letter was written there was more tragedy in the Dickens household for his loyal dog, a bull mastiff named Turk, was killed on the railway, hit by a train and it must have seemed as if the railways were tormenting and haunting him.

In the days after the crash he continually wrote about being shocked and affected by the memories of the scenes he had witnessed during the rescue effort, but later it was the physical memories of the crash itself that would plague him, and his children were greatly concerned. Mamie wrote that he would 'suddenly fall into a paroxysm of fear, tremble all over, clutch the arms of the railway carriage, large beads of perspiration standing on his face, and suffer agonies of terror. We never spoke to him but would touch his hand gently now and then. He had, apparently, no idea of our presence; he saw nothing for a time but that most awful scene. Sometimes he would get better, and sometimes the agony was so great, he had to get out at the nearest station and walk home. I remember this happening twice.' And Charles himself confirmed a few years after the crash that 'to this hour I have sudden vague rushes of terror, which are perfectly unreasonable, but quite insurmountable'.

Throughout the remaining years of his life he would travel extensively and many of the letters to his family, as well as his closest confidants such as Forster and Wills, spoke of his fear and discomfort on the trains; gradually those fears would subside but towards the end of his life the terrors returned and haunted him once more.

Throughout 1865 he completed *Our Mutual Friend* and accompanying the final number, published in November of that year, Charles included a short postscript written directly to his readers acknowledging the fact that the characters of the novel had been travelling with him on the fateful day:

'On Friday the Ninth of June in the present year, Mr and Mrs Boffin (in their manuscript dress of receiving Mr and Mrs Lammle at breakfast) were on the South Eastern Railway with me in a terribly destructive accident. When I had done what I could to help others, I climbed back into my carriage — nearly turned over a viaduct, and caught aslant upon the turn — to extricate the worthy couple. They were much soiled, but otherwise unhurt. The same happy result attended Miss Bella Wilfer on her wedding day, and Mr Riderhood inspecting Bradley Headstone's red neckerchief as he lay asleep. I remember with devout thankfulness that I can never be nearer parting company with my readers forever, than I was then, until there shall be written against my life, the two words with which I have this day closed this book: — THE END.'

In 1866 with pressures of producing *Our Mutual Friend* behind him Charles was able to resume his reading career and it is very interesting to compare the schedule of his last major UK tour which had spanned 1861 to 1863, to the new one. On the earlier occasion he had left London on 28th October '61 and travelled to Norwich, Bury St Edmunds, Ipswich, Colchester, Canterbury, Dover, Hastings, Brighton, Newcastle-upon-Tyne, Berwick, Edinburgh, Glasgow, Carlisle, Lancaster, Preston, Manchester, Birmingham, Leamington, Cheltenham, Plymouth, Torquay, Exeter, Manchester, Liverpool and Chester before returning home to London for the first time. It was a mammoth undertaking and bespoke a man tormented by his fractured home life and craving the adulation of his readers.

In 1866, with Ellen safely installed in Slough and a sense of stability returning to his life, the tour was planned differently: Cheltenham. Back to London. Liverpool and Manchester, Glasgow and Edinburgh. Back to London. Manchester and Liverpool again. Back to London. Clifton, Birmingham. Back to London. Aberdeen, Glasgow, Edinburgh. Back to London and so on. The opportunities for Charles to visit 'Mrs Tringham' in Slough were much more frequent.

The reading tours were only made possible by the railway system, so Charles had to conquer his fears and memories of Staplehurst on an almost daily basis and in Ellen he had not only a loving companion but also someone who had shared the same experience, who understood, who could listen and comfort him when the nightmares returned.

Although they could never be together in the conventional sense, Charles and Ellen continued their secret life as Mr and Mrs Tringham first in Slough and later in a larger house in Peckham (once more with convenient rail links to both the centre of London and Gad's Hill Place).

The first anniversary of the accident passed without mention in Dickens' letters, for his correspondence from Gad's Hill Place concentrated on business affairs, but he must surely have felt a pang of fear as he read the newspaper reports of a great rail crash in the Welwyn Tunnel which occurred on June 9th, 1866.

Twenty miles north of London, on the King's Cross Line, is Welwyn station, and a little further on there are two tunnels, the North and the South. In 1866 a lone signalman, was placed at the entrance of the first tunnel to ensure that the 'all clear' signal was not given until a train had passed through safely.

At 11:20 pm on the night of June 9th an empty coal train made its way safely through the first tunnel having left the station, but when it was about halfway through the second it rolled to a halt, due to a steam supply pipe bursting in the boiler. On the train were the driver and the stoker, Mr Wray, as well as another railwayman, Mr Rawlins, who was taking a ride home, disobeying company regulations in doing so. It was Wray's duty, in such a circumstance to make his way towards the mouth of the tunnel laying detonators along the track to act as a warning to any train that may be coming on behind. In an oversight with awful echoes of Staplehurst Wray did not place the charges, so that when another goods train loaded with oil and tallow sped into the tunnel there was no warning for the driver. The collision that followed was so violent that it shattered the brake van and scattered debris across the upline. At the same time a third train entered the tunnel from the opposite direction and collided with the debris from the initial collision, blocking the bore completely. The fires from the three boilers then ignited the flammable load of the second train and there was an explosion of gargantuan proportions. The ventilation shaft through the roof of the tunnel acted as a flue and provided perfect conditions for a conflagration that could not be extinguished for two days.

The fact that the three trains involved had all been goods trains meant that the loss of life was small. The stoker, Wray, was killed at the scene, whilst Rawlings the unofficial passenger died from his injuries two days later.

When the Board of Trade report was published the name affixed to the bottom was FH Rich, RE, the same gentleman who had reported on Staplehurst.

Whether the news reports of the Welwyn crash awoke

Dickens' memories is not certain, but when he began to think about his Christmas edition of *All The Year Round* for 1866 his thoughts turned to the railway for his subject matter. *Mugby Junction* was a collection of stories featuring a narrator by the name of Jackson enjoying his recent retirement by travelling the rail network. Three of the stories in the collection were written by Dickens and the others by various other authors which were 'of undulating quality' as Robert McFarlane politely points out in the foreword to his 2005 edition of the collection.

The fourth story is *The Signalman* in which Jackson happens upon a lonely signal box in a deep railway cutting manned by a solitary and lonely signalman. From the outset the language is dark and doom-laden: 'His post was in as solitary and dismal a place as ever I saw. On either side, a dripping-wet wall of jagged stone, excluding all view but a strip of sky; the perspective one way only a crooked prolongation of this great dungeon; the shorter perspective in the other direction terminating in a gloomy red light, and the gloomier entrance to a black tunnel, in whose massive architecture there was a barbarous, depressing, and forbidding air. So little sunlight ever found its way to this spot, that it had an earthy, deadly smell; and so much cold wind rushed through it, that it struck chill to me, as if I had left the natural world.'

The signalman invites Jackson into his hut and proceeds to describe a series of hauntings at the tunnel's mouth, each of which precedes a tragic and disastrous calamity. The first accident was a crash deep within the tunnel and for hours afterwards the dead and the wounded were carried from the scene, as the casualties at Staplehurst had been pulled from the river by the author himself.

Following the second haunting the distraught signalman

tells how 'a beautiful young lady had died instantaneously in one of the compartments, and was brought in here, and laid down on this floor between us', mirroring Dickens' experience on the banks of the Beult when he and his fellow rescuer had witnessed a fine and handsome lady being pulled from the river having been crushed to death. 'She was laid out on the bank.'

Dickens didn't simply re-tell the story of Staplehurst in fictionalised form, for a bridge with an elevation of only ten feet above a dry riverbed is hardly the stuff of terrifying ghost stories, but the demons behind the tale were real enough. In fact, the setting was probably taken from the scene of yet another rail crash, at Clayton Tunnel near Brighton where 23 people had lost their lives in 1861 as two trains collided following a signalling malfunction, and which certainly matches the dour gothic description.

The Clayton Tunnel

The Clayton Tunnel crash had actually been caused by a failure of the block signalling system, allowing two trains to be on a single track at the same time. In *The Signalman* Dickens accurately described the 'telegraphic instrument with its dial, face and needle' as well as the electric bell that sounded the alerts (indeed, the bell becomes a supernatural character in the narrative as do the telegraph wires that moan mournfully in the wind). It is obvious that Dickens had carefully studied the system and, in all likelihood, read the detailed reports of the Clayton crash to infuse his words with a sense of realism.

The writing of *Mugby Junction* was not solely the result of the twin tragedies of Staplehurst and losing his dog, Turk, for Dickens had been travelling extensively on the railway system during his reading tours and had many experiences on which to draw. His tour manager George Dolby in his book *Charles Dickens, As I Knew Him* recalled one occasion when Dickens was travelling; he entered '...the refreshment-room, he and Mr Wills had each asked for a cup of coffee, which was supplied to them. While Wills was feeling in his pocket for some small change wherewith to pay, Mr Dickens reached across the counter for the sugar and milk, when both articles were suddenly snatched away from him and placed beneath the counter, while his ears were greeted with the remark made in shrill and shrewish tones, "You shan't have any milk and sugar till you fellows have paid for your coffee!"'

The first scene in *The Boy at Mugby* is in a railway refreshment room 'what's proudest boast is, that it never yet refreshed a mortal being'.

The *Mugby Junction* collection of stories sold very well; on the 28th December Dickens wrote that it had 'turned

250,000' and the success moved him to prepare readings from them, to introduce into his repertoire for his ongoing tours. He 'worked up' three scripts, *The Barbox Brothers*, *The Boy at Mugby Junction* and *The Signalman*, but only the former two made it to performance. Why did he never perform *The Signalman*? I think there are two reasons, one being that the memories associated with it continued to torment him and it may well have been that he was seized with uncontrollable spasms of fear as he rehearsed it. The second reason is, I suggest, a more practical decision of a theatrical man: the script was not a long one, a little more than thirty minutes, and it would only be useful as a 'short' to be performed after the main event of an evening. Typically, the shorter readings were light and comedic, such as 'The Trial' from *Pickwick* or 'Mrs Gamp' from *Martin Chuzzelwit* and they were designed to send an audience home in good humour; it may well have been that Dickens felt that such a dark story was not appropriate for the purpose.

Whatever the reason for abandoning the idea of reading *The Signalman* the other pieces from the collection didn't last long either. *The Barbox Brothers* and *The Boy* were first performed in London on January 15th, 1867 and, according to Dolby '…justified the misgivings felt at rehearsal. It was received cordially by the audience, but it was apparent that it would never rank with the other works of its kind.'

Dolby opined that Dickens 'was conscious of this, and but for the fact that the reading was already announced for some of the towns in the early part of the tour, it is probable that *Barbox* and *The Boy* would have been shelved there and then.'

As it was, the double bill faded from the repertoire as early as February.

The secret relationship with Ellen continued. In the

summer of 1867 Mr Tringham settled a new lease on the larger house in Peckham and paid regular visits to his 'wife' there. Plans were in place for another trip to America, this time for a reading tour, and the idea came to the couple that it would be a wonderful and liberating thing if Ellen could travel with Charles, although he feared how a country with vociferously conservative morals would react to her. Eventually he decided to travel alone and gauge the situation when he arrived. In the meantime, Ellen was safely away from London, living in Italy, waiting to hear whether she would travel to America or not.

Shortly before his departure in November he confirmed the arrangements he had made as part of a general memorandum to Wills, under the sub-heading 'Nelly'. He wrote, 'If she needs any help will come to you, or if she changes her address, you will immediately let me know if she changes. Until then it will be Villa Trollope, à Ricorboli, Firenze, Italy.

'On the day after my arrival out I will send you a short telegram at the office. Please copy its exact words (as they will have a special meaning for her) and post them to her as above by the very next post after receiving my telegram. And also let Gad's Hill know — and let Forster know — what the telegram is.'

When it arrived from Boston the telegram was worded in such a way as to let Ellen know that she was to remain in Florence before returning to England. Mr and Mrs Tringham would not be reunited on American soil after all.

By this time Charles was in poor health and suffered throughout the American trip, eschewing appearances and invitations away from his performance commitments. If Ellen had travelled with him, she would have been a nurse and companion for an ailing man whose photographs show a figure of much greater years than his 56.

Charles Dickens in New York, 1867

During the trip Dickens constantly wrote home gleefully recounting how successful the tour was, both artistically and financially, and in many letters to the trusted Wills he enclosed notes to be forwarded to Ellen with requests for the glowing newspaper reports of his performances to be sent to her also.

As in England the constant rail travel played on his mind, and in one letter to John Forster he wrote that 'the railways are truly alarming. Much worse (because more worn I suppose) than when I was here before. We were beaten about yesterday, as if we had been aboard the *Cuba* (the ship on which he had crossed the Atlantic).

'Two rivers have to be crossed, and each time the whole train is banged aboard a big steamer. The steamer rises and falls with the river, which the railroad doesn't do; and the train is either banged uphill or banged downhill. In coming off the steamer at one of these crossings yesterday, we were banged up such a height that the rope broke, and one carriage rushed back with a run downhill into the boat again. I whisked out in a moment, and two or three others after me; but nobody else seemed to care about it.'

The other issue that plagued him throughout the journey was a constant cold in the head, which he blamed on the snowy, icy conditions and the stuffy heat of the railway cars. In almost every letter home he gave both a meteorological and medical bulletin ('The weather has been desperately severe, and my cold quite as bad as ever'), and on many occasions he remained in his hotel room throughout the day, emerging only to perform at night.

The effects of the American reading tour would be long-lasting and profound, and he was still writing about them years later; for example, in one letter written in the spring of 1870 he stated that 'I am very sorry that I cannot have the pleasure of accepting your kind invitation. But I am occasionally subject to a Neuralgic (or whatever else it may be) attack in the foot, which originated a few years ago, in over-walking in deep snow, and was revived by a very hard winter in America; and it has so plagued me, under the dinings and other engagements of this London Season, that I have been lame these three weeks, and have resolved on an absolute rest in Kent here, and an avoidance of hot rooms, and an unbroken quiet training, for some months.'

The American tour ended in April 1868 and he was finally able to return to England; financially the trip had been a huge success, but he was exhausted and frail from the extreme exertions he had placed upon himself.

Despite his physical frailties Charles still filled his life and worked with a zeal and energy that would floor much younger men. During the continuing readings he threw himself into his performances to such an extent that often he collapsed afterwards and was forced to lie on the sofa until he recovered. As he performed, Dolby watched from the wings, and often members of his family were in the audience too to keep an eye on him. Pushing himself ever further he decided to introduce a new reading into his repertoire, more energetic and dramatic than anything that had gone before. For a number of years, he had been experimenting with a performance based around the murder of Nancy from his second novel, *Oliver Twist*. Those around him, Forster, Dolby and the family pleaded with him not to attempt the piece, but he was stubborn and in the early days of 1869 *Sikes and Nancy* was unleashed onto the public.

Initially the critical reaction was lukewarm, to say the least: 'Mr Dickens is a great reader, but he is much more gracious in the rendering of other passages than the murder episode from the least worthy of his books. In the hands of a less accomplished and gifted reader the rendering would be disgusting.'

Performing Sikes and Nancy in 1869

Another reporter whilst praising the performance saw no future in the reading, noting that 'the recital was terribly impressive, but some of the ladies in the stalls were obviously shocked. I don't think that Mr Dickens will repeat the experiment. The story is very ghastly and there is no useful moral in it. These readings of the great novelist are now drawing to a close, and the public will never hear the voice of 'Boz' again. Mr Dickens announces the series as his last, and when Mr Dickens says a thing, he does it. He is not a man to indulge in 'more last appearances'.' The final comment being a wry nod towards the Crummles Theatre Company from Charles's third novel *Nicholas Nickleby*. The reporter in question was obviously not fully furnished with the facts, for the report was filed on 15th January 1869 and Dickens would still be touring, and performing *Sikes and Nancy*, over a year later.

At one of the early performances Dickens invited his old friend William Charles Macready to attend. The great actor manager who had played all of the great roles on all of the great stages was now frail and in poor health but keen to support his dear friend. Charles sat him in the front row so that he could see and hear everything. Following the show, the tragedian exclaimed, 'It comes to this — er — two Macbeths!' Dickens said that Macready had said this with extraordinary energy, '...after which he stood (with his glass in his hand and his old square jaw of its old fierce form) looking defiantly at Dolby as if Dolby had contradicted him; and then trailed off into a weak pale likeness of himself, as if his whole appearance had been some clever optical illusion'.

In spirit Dickens was as passionate as ever but in body he

was weak, and even as early as February his doctors were concerned. In a letter to Forster Dickens told him the news that the surgeon Sir Henry Thompson 'will not let me read to-night, and will not let me go to Scotland to-morrow.

'Tremendous house here, and also in Edinburgh. Here is the certificate he drew up for himself and Beard to sign. "We the undersigned hereby certify that Mr. C. D. is suffering from inflammation of the foot (caused by over-exertion), and that we have forbidden his appearance on the platform this evening, as he must keep his room for a day or two." I have sent up to the Great Western Hotel for apartments, and, if I can get them, shall move there this evening. Heaven knows what engagements this may involve in April! It throws us all back, and will cost me some five hundred pounds.'

Rather than worrying about April Dickens was actually back on the stage at the end of February, writing to Wills that 'I have been getting on exceedingly well with my foot, so far. Although I feel it a little fatigued by the standing at night, it has caused me no other inconvenience. "Business" here is tremendous!', and to Mamie, 'The foot goes famously, I feel the fatigue in it (four murders in one week) but not overmuch. It merely aches at night; and so does the other, sympathetically, I suppose.' Four murders in a week was not the action of a man trying to save himself.

Unfortunately, the performance was such a huge hit with audiences that it became the talking point of the tour, meaning that Dickens could not stint on his commitments: everyone wanted to see the great man commit murder and he satiated their desire, at the expense of his own health.

His final touring dates for 1869 would be in April and it is noticeable that his letters during this time were not as ebullient as usual. They seem to speak of a man on the point of exhaustion; his swollen foot was still a source of worry to him, 'We have a large Let at Bradford tonight, and our five-shilling tickets for tomorrow night here are advertised in the newspapers at a guinea each. We came down through a heavy thunder-storm. The foot was bad all the way, and was exceedingly inflamed and swollen when we arrived, and still is. But I had a splendid night. I regret to say that the foot is certainly no better this morning. It naturally makes us very anxious.'

And then, out of the blue came news from Mark Lemon, the editor of *Punch* who had acted in *The Frozen Deep* alongside Dickens and Ellen which awoke old demons in Dickens. On 16th April he wrote:

'My Dear Lemon

I send you a hasty line to let you know that I have had your messages to day, and that I am heartily glad to know that you were but very slightly shaken by your "Railway accident". The phrase has had a dreadful significance to me, ever since the Staplehurst occasion. Be sure that you do right in being as quiet as you can.'

With the memories of Staplehurst awoken again Charles Dickens must have been heartily glad that his touring days, using the express trains to travel the length and breadth of the country, were soon to end. 'I am half dead with travelling every day and reading afterwards. As much of me as is alive, sends its love.

'I don't wonder at the Papers being confused regarding my whereabout, when I am confused myself! I am in a different place every day and shall have no rest until after the 12th of June, when I finish for good and all in London.'

Actually his final performance of 1869 would be on the 20th April in Bolton, for among his letters during that week were two obviously fearful ones to his private physician, Doctor Frank Beard, 'Is it *possible* that anything in my medicine can have made me extremely giddy, extremely uncertain of my footing (especially on the left side) and extremely indisposed to raise my hands to my head? These symptoms made me very uncomfortable on Saturday night, and all yesterday. I have taken the medicine twice a day only and have taken barely a bottle in all.

'If you can, send me one word in answer by return, to the Imperial Hotel, Blackpool, do.'

Two days later he wrote again, 'I received your kind note on coming here this afternoon. As you evidently thought the symptoms worthy of immediate attention, I at once telegraphed to you my tomorrow's and Friday's addresses. The said symptoms have greatly moderated since Sunday: but there they are, and they are all on the left side. Six weeks will carry me through the Readings, if you can fortify me a little bit, and then please God I may do as I like.'

To his nearest and dearest he admitted his fears but seemed for a few days still intent on continuing with the tour; to Forster he said, 'Don't say anything about it, but the tremendously severe nature of this work is a little shaking me. At Chester last Sunday I found myself extremely giddy, and extremely uncertain of my sense of touch, both in the left leg and the left hand and arms. I had been taking some slight medicine of Beard's; and immediately wrote to him describing exactly what I felt, and asking him whether those feelings *could be* referable to the medicine? He promptly replied: "There can be no mistaking them from your exact account. The medicine cannot possibly have caused them. I recognise indisputable symptoms of overwork, and I wish to take you in hand without any loss of time." They have greatly modified since, but he is coming down here this afternoon. To-morrow night and Warrington I shall have but 25 more nights to work through. If he can coach me up for them, I do not doubt that I shall get all right again — as I did when I became free in America.'

Beard understood the severity of his patient's condition; the paralysis on the left side bespoke a stroke, or series of mini-strokes, with the imminent danger of a major haemorrhage to the brain. He gently advised Charles Dickens to return home with no further exertion.

Chapel and Co, the company who funded and promoted the tours, assured Dickens that there would be no financial penalty due to the cancellations, and along with George Dolby they began the process of informing the venues and the public that the tour was ended.

Of course, with the pressures of travelling and performing removed Dickens' health recovered quickly. Dolby mentioned that 'I was most pleasurably surprised at seeing him, and more than this, for all traces of his illness had disappeared. In his light suit of clothes and round hat, carried jauntily on the side of his head, he looked the picture of health. He was very much sunburnt, and although I had only parted from him a few days previously, the change in him was so great that I hardly believed I saw before me the man who had looked so haggard and worn but five or six weeks ago.'

To his American publisher and one of his closest friends from Boston, James Fields, Charles wrote in reassurance that 'I fear you will have been uneasy about me, and will have heard distorted accounts of the stoppage of my Readings. It is a measure of precaution, and not of cure. I was too tired, and too jarred by the Railway fast express travelling night and day. No half measure could be taken; and rest being medically considered essential, we stopped.' And to Thomas Adolphus Trollope he also mentioned that the continual jolting of the express trains had proved too difficult to bear. The fear of rail travel, and the ghosts of Staplehurst, still weighed heavily on him four years after the crash.

Throughout the summer his health and spirts recovered remarkably and he delighted in galivanting around London with Mr Fields and his wife Annie who were visiting. Indeed, the schedule for their activities took up as much of his time as his writing or performing had in the past.

When Mr and Mrs Fields bade their farewells and returned to America Dickens became frustrated once more. As was natural for a man of his immense energy he became restless, comparing himself at one point to a caged lion at the Regent's Park Zoo. With so much time at home (Charles Jnr had taken over the day to day management of *All The Year Round* with Wills) it is not surprising that thoughts turned to the creation of a new novel, the first since *Our Mutual Friend* had been completed in 1865.

In July 1869 he wrote to Forster, 'What should you think of the idea of a story beginning in this way? — Two people, boy and girl, or very young, going apart from one another, pledged to be married after many years — at the end of the book. The interest to arise out of the tracing of their separate ways, and the impossibility of telling what will be done with that impending fate.'

The Mystery of Edwin Drood had been born and it was destined to outlive its creator.

He also agreed with Chapels to resume his farewell readings, on the understanding that all the performances would be in London, thereby necessitating no express rail travel. A series of dates was booked for January and February 1870 at the St James' Hall and once more the publicity machine rolled into action, whilst at Gad's Hill, and presumably Peckham, he began to rehearse once more.

Early in 1870 he had been invited to The Birmingham and Midland Institute to award prizes, and still the travel disturbed him; 'am a little shaken by my journey to Birmingham to give away the Institution's prizes on Twelfth Night', he wrote to John Forster, but most of his time was spent safely at home working on *Drood* and rehearsing for the forthcoming readings. The new schedule was not too punishing, the twelve performances spread over three months with only one or two each week. Doctor Beard, George Dolby and the Dickens family went to great lengths to ensure that Charles didn't over-exert himself (at one of the final readings Charley was sat in the front row so that he could catch his father should he collapse and stumble and remove him from the stage, 'or,' as Beard warned, 'he will die before them all!').

Considering the fragility of Dickens' health, it is surprising that he was allowed to perform *Sikes and Nancy* as part of these final readings, but there it was in his schedule and in particular he gave 'The Murder' at a specially arranged matinee for theatre folk at which Ellen was present. He had always loved surrounding himself with fellow actors and he craved the adulation that his knowledgeable audience would surely give him. He wrote to Wills that 'the actors and actresses (most of the latter looking very pretty) mustered in extra-ordinary force, and were a fine audience. I set myself to carrying out of themselves and their observation, those who were bent on watching how the effects were got: — and I believe I succeeded.'

The letter continued as Dickens admitted the ridiculous strain that he put on himself, 'Coming back to it again, however, I feel it was madness ever to do it continuously. My ordinary pulse is 72, and it runs up under this effort to 112. Besides which, it takes me ten or twelve minutes to get my wind back at all.' He finished by alluding to Ellen, who was well known to Wills, 'The patient was in attendance and missed you. I was charged with all manner of good and kind remembrance.' As part of the secretive code in which Charles wrote of Ellen, she had been known as 'the patient' since she had broken her arm at Staplehurst.

The final performance was given on March 15th and on that evening he performed the two pieces that had formed the mainstay of his reading career and which were particular favourites with both the performer and the reader, *A Christmas Carol* and *The Trial* from *Pickwick*. The momentous significance of the event ensured a packed house and the audience hung on every word and cheered him to the rafters (despite the fact that he struggled throughout the latter part of the evening finding himself unable to pronounce the name of Pickwick, coming out with various attempts such as 'Pecknicks' and 'Pickswick').

George Dolby watched the 'Guv'nor' from his customary place from the side of the platform, and in his memoir gives a real sense of the emotion of that night:

'The final farewell reading…was one of the hardest struggles he had to face, but he went through it with a manliness and good temper which eclipsed all his previous efforts.

'Mr Dickens walked on to the platform, book in hand. But evidently much agitated. He was thinking, I dare say, that this was to be the very last time he would address an audience in his capacity of reader…But no feeling of sadness could have been retained in face of the unanimity and splendour of the reception that was accorded him. The immense audience rose to their feet and cheered him to the echo. This lasted some minutes. In spontaneity and warmth, it was a provincial rather than a metropolitan reception. It had the instant effect of nerving him up to his work, and he never read The Carol more earnestly, more fervently, or more effectively than on this occasion. The audience, needless to say, were in supreme sympathy with the reader. Not a word was lost. They seemed to feel that they were hearing him for the last time.'

At the end of the two readings the audience's reaction was loud, vociferous and prolonged. 'He had responded several times to the calls for his reappearance,' Dolby continued, 'but seemed anxious to defer as long as possible the few words of farewell he had mentally prepared. But it had to be done, and, nerving himself up for the crowning effort, he returned once more to the little table (for the last time and for ever), and with a voice full of emotion, and amid breathless silence, he spoke…'

In the respectful hush of the hall, Dickens thanked his audiences of fifteen years, he remembered to mention that his new novel would be available in just two weeks' time (ever the businessman) and then concluded by saying 'but from these garish lights I vanish now for evermore, with a heartfelt, grateful, respectful, and affectionate farewell'.

The reading tours that had dominated his professional life during his last years were at an end.

Throughout the rest of March, April and May he worked hard at *The Mystery of Edwin Drood*, the first instalment of which was published shortly after his final reading in London. The book is mainly set in the fictional town of Cloisterham which is a thinly disguised representation of Rochester, the city in which Charles had played as a boy; the city where the members of The Pickwick Club had travelled at the beginning of their adventures, staying in The Bull Hotel; the city where Pip had visited Miss Havisham at Satis House and received his indentures in the great Guildhall. The city where Ellen Lawless Ternan had been born.

Throughout these few months his health continued to trouble him. In May he wrote to Forster, 'I am sorry to report that, in the old preposterous endeavour to dine at preposterous hours and preposterous places, I have been pulled up by a sharp attack in my foot. And serve me right. I hope to get the better of it soon, but I fear I must not think of dining with you on Friday. I have cancelled everything in the dining way for this week, and that is a very small precaution after the horrible pain I have had and the remedies I have taken.' And to Mrs Fitzgerald, 'I have been subject for a few years past to a Neuralgic attack in the foot, originating in over-walking in deep snow and revived by a hard winter in America. For the last three weeks it has made me dead-lame, and it now obliges me to beg absolution from all the social engagements I had made.'

By June the first twelve chapters of *Drood* had been published and on the morning of Monday 6th Charles was still working hard in the little Swiss chalet which had been a gift from his friend, and fellow actor, Charles Fechter. Sitting on the upper floor, amongst the trees, he delighted in having the windows wide open so that he could hear birdsong and allow the butterflies and bees to come and go as they pleased.

As he worked his two daughters Mary and Katey were due to leave Gad's Hill. Usually they would have left without disturbing their father but on this occasion, Katey turned back.

'I MUST say goodbye to Papa,' she told her sister and ran back to the chalet. Rather than his customary response of offering his cheek to be kissed on this occasion Dickens turned to his daughter and held her in his arms saying, 'God Bless you, Katey.' He told her that he had wished he had been a better father, a better man. And she parted with him for the last time.

On Wednesday 8th June he was back in the chalet, not only continuing with the novel but also writing his inevitable correspondence, including a letter to Charles Kent whom he hoped to meet in London the next day. Prophetically he wrote, 'Tomorrow is a very bad day for me to make a call, as in addition to my usual office business, I have a mass of accounts to settle with Wills. But I hope I may be ready for you at 3 o'clock. If I can't be — why, then I shan't be.'

In the evening he took dinner in the dining room with his sister-in-law Georgina Hogarth and she noticed that he looked to be in pain. She asked him if he had been ill and he replied, 'Yes, very ill; I have been ill for the last hour.' Even as he spoke the massive developing stroke caused his next words to be fragmented and largely incoherent. He spoke of needing to travel to London and tried to stand but immediately stumbled into Georgina's arms. She was hardly strong enough to support him and he whispered, 'on the ground.' The great wordsmith had delivered his final speech.

Local doctors were sent for, as was Doctor Beard from London. Telegrams were sent to his daughters Mamie and Katey and his sons Charley and Henry who made their way home to the house that Charles had admired as a nine-year-old boy. He was lifted onto a sofa which was brought into the dining room and throughout the night he breathed deeply without regaining consciousness. On Thursday 9th June his family, including Ellen who had been called from Peckham, maintained their vigil. It was obvious that there could be no saving him and it was simply a matter of time.

Mamie wrote, 'We watched all through the night, and all through the next day, but he never once opened his eyes, or showed one sign of consciousness. It was better so for him. The last "good bye" would have caused him so much pain and sorrow. But we could tell the moment — ten minutes past six — when his spirit took flight. A shadow stole across his face, a tear rolled down his cheek, he gave a deep sigh, and he was gone from us.'

Charles Dickens died on 9th June 1870: five years, to the very day, after the tidal train had plunged into the River Beult near Staplehurst.

The Empty Chair by Luke Fieldes, taken from a sketch made at Gad's Hill Place on 10 June 1870

CHARLES DICKENS AND POST-TRAUMATIC STRESS DISORDER

When considering Charles Dickens' reaction to the crash at Staplehurst it seems inevitable that he was suffering from a form of Post-Traumatic Stress Disorder. Although PTSD is often seen as a modern phenomenon there are certain historical incidents that are commonly quoted; one is Samuel Pepys' nightmares and insomnia after witnessing the Great Fire of London in 1666 and another is that of Charles Dickens in 1865.

In his book *PTSD. Horror in the Mind* Mark Tyrrell states that the origins of the condition stem from the human's need to survive, in particular his ability to learn from experience. He writes, 'Cast your mind back a few thousand years and imagine a tribal man wandering across a barren plain into a crop of trees.

'Suddenly, he becomes aware of the movement of grass at the base of a tree. He barely has time to register the motion before a snarling lion pounces upon him.

'Paralysed with fear, he knows there is no escape. Death feels certain. Then, just in the nick of time, his tribe appears to rescue him. Physically, the damage is minimal — he survives with a few lacerations and grazes. But mentally, the learning experience was deep.

'A month later, his wounds have healed completely. He is

walking through some trees with his fellow tribe members, far from where the incident occurred. Just then a gust of wind rustles through the grass at the base of a tree and, much to the surprise of his unsuspecting tribe, he screams and runs, shaking and sweating.

'He reacted *as if* those different trees were the same trees as before, *as if* the movement in the grass was again caused by a lion, *as if* he was going to be mauled.

'You see, to maximise our chances of survival the mind needs to err on the side of caution. Your brain needs to make sloppy matches in that way in order to keep you alive.

'The part of the brain in control of this process is the amygdala, which is deeply involved with memory processing, emotions, and decision-making — but not logic! That means that anything that even vaguely reminds the brain of the original trauma sets off the flight or fight reaction again.'

Charles Dickens could easily be cast as Tyrrell's imagined tribal survivor in the sense that the trauma was completely unexpected, resulted in no physical harm and yet the triggers to fear, and survival, were firmly implanted in his brain.

In the upturned carriage his brain processed the knowledge that he had survived quickly, for he immediately told Ellen and her mother that 'you may be sure nothing worse can happen. Our danger *must* be over.' His composure was remarkable and the violence of the crash did not seem to weigh heavily on him. Indeed, in the many letters he wrote in the days following, he was at pains to repeat that he 'was not touched — scarcely shaken'. The initial trauma stemmed from the awful sights he had seen as he joined in the rescue effort: the dead, mutilated and terribly wounded figures that affected him deeply. In his description there was a sense of helplessness, especially as the first passengers that he tried to help were either dead or died in his arms.

In modern cases of PTSD patients who have escaped and witnessed death, i.e. soldiers who have lost comrades, speak not of a fear of being back at the scene but a reality. Tyrrell quotes such a soldier as stating that if he is out shopping and he hears 'a siren wailing from the street, or even the crash of a slammed door, or a car backfiring, or distant youths shouting, or the smell of smoke and I'm right back there. It's not just a memory; it's like I'm actually back there again. I feel I am about to die. There are no thoughts; just feelings. My war should have finished. It hasn't, though. I can't live like this.'

That response is exactly as Mamie and Henry both describe, when they recalled that their father '...had no idea of our presence; he saw nothing for a time but that awful scene. Sometimes he would suddenly get better, and sometimes the agony was so great, he had to get out at the nearest station and walk home.' Like the soldier Charles was not only remembering the crash but actually re-living it: he was back at Staplehurst with the carriage being dragged along like the ground 'as the car of a half-emptied balloon might'.

By returning to rail travel so soon (he would take a train from London to Higham just days after the crash) he indirectly undertook what is known as 'exposure therapy', in effect getting back on the horse, and to an extent it worked, but he often abandoned journeys on express services in favour of slower local trains. Over a year and a half after the initial trauma he was fearing for his life once more and felt the need to 'go public' by writing an indignant letter to *The Times* newspaper:

'Sir,

As it is better to prevent a horrible accident by a timely caution than sagaciously to observe after its occurrence that anyone acquainted with the circumstances out of which it arose could have easily foreseen it, I beg most earnestly to warn the public through your columns against the morning express train on the Midland railway between Leicester and Bedford.

'I took that train this morning, leaving Leicester at 9:35. The reckless fury of the driving and the violent rocking of the carriages obliged me to leave it at Bedford rather than come on to London with my through ticket. When we stopped at Market Harborough general alarm was expressed by the passengers, and strong remonstrances were urged on the officials, also, at Bedford. I am an experienced railway traveller at home and abroad; I was in the Staplehurst accident; I have been in trains under most conceivable conditions, but I have never been so shaken and flung about as in this train, and have never been in such obvious danger.

'The very obliging authorities suggested that the road was "rough" from the thaw, and that I was in a light carriage. As to the first suggestion, I am certain from experience on other railways since the thaw set in that there is no such "roughness" on other railways. As to the second, one of the passengers who protested the most strongly was a gentleman in a heavy carriage next to my own.

'I may add that my companion in the carriage (who left the train with me) is almost constantly on English railways, and fully confirms what I have here written.'

Your faithful servant, Charles Dickens

It is clear that his mind was still reliving Staplehurst and even that he felt the need to 'save' his fellow travellers as he had tried to do in 1865.

Over the years Dickens' symptoms of PTSD began to fade (which is usual) as his hectic lifestyle made greater demands upon him. Other fears for his life, especially in respect of his ever-worsening gout, overwhelmed his thoughts, but it only took the slightest trigger to take him back to the carriage hanging over the bridge above the Beult, and the letter from Mark Lemon in 1869 speaking of his involvement in a derailment was such a trigger and from the time the pain of travel increased once more and the horrors returned. His final public appearance in Birmingham called for a rail journey and as we have already seen he wrote to Forster telling him that he was unnerved by the experience. Every rattle, every sway, every shudder and every whistle became the rustling of the grass at the base of the tree and deep in his psyche the primeval need to survive took over his mind and his body.

There is some evidence that those who suffer from persisting PTSD are often people who are particularly imaginative and prone to hypnosis, both of which sum up Charles Dickens perfectly. His imagination, of course, is clear to the millions of people who have read his books over the years, but he was also a great student of mesmerism, as hypnosis was known in the 19th century. As early as 1838, glowing in the success of *Pickwick*, he had attended a display of mesmerism at the University College Hospital and was spellbound as Doctor John Elliotson hypnotised a young woman. Dickens was astounded by what he saw and was in no doubt as to the reality of the scene; this was no circus sideshow. A confirmed sceptic prior to the demonstration Charles became not only a believer but a fervent promoter of the science. He studied every book that he could find upon the subject and convinced Elliotson to teach him the techniques required to practise. Over the years Dickens successfully hypnotised Catherine, Georgina and many of his friends, proving his hypnotic nature.

With such a fertile mind it is certainly no surprise that Charles Dickens should have been so susceptible to the terrors and memories that overwhelmed him.

A few years ago, after a performance of *The Signalman*, a member of the audience approached me and quietly told me that my account of Charles Dickens' continuing terrors had resonated with him particularly, for he himself had been involved in the Ladbroke Grove train crash in October 1999 and the day haunted him still. He kindly offered to talk to me about his memories, although he knew that they would be painful, and invited me to his house where we sat in his quiet study. Coincidentally, and appropriately, we were watched over by an old engraving depicting Sam and Tony Weller from *The Pickwick Papers*. After a short pause Peter began to talk.

The facts of Ladbroke Grove are that during the morning of October 5, 1999, a local train left Paddington Station in west London bound for Bedwyn in Wiltshire. The stretch of line from Paddington to Ladbroke Grove was bi-directional, meaning that trains could travel in either direction on the same track, rather than the more traditional method of separate 'up' and 'down' lines. As the Bedwyn train approached the Ladbroke Grove area a red signal was displayed warning the driver to stop, as there was an express train travelling into London on the same track. For whatever reason the driver, Michael Hodder, who had only recently completed his training, missed the light and continued onto the track straight into the path of the 6:03 from Cheltenham. It was 8:09 in the morning. The collision was catastrophic, destroying the front of the local train and flinging the express from the rails. Diesel oil from ruptured fuel lines was ignited and a series of fireballs engulfed the wreckage. 31 people were killed (including both drivers) and 417 others were injured.

Peter had been a passenger in the rearmost coach of the express, the so-called 'quiet' coach and was making his daily commute into London where he worked for one of the major banks. He was a typical commuter on a typical commuter train, exchanging polite glances with his fellow travellers with whom he shared the journey every day. He remembers that the train seemed to be quieter that morning, and that a pregnant woman who usually boarded at Reading and relied on the gallantry of other passengers for a seat, was not on the train on October 5th, ensuring a providential escape for her and her unborn child.

As the train neared Paddington station Peter glanced at his watch. It read 8:03, and he stood to retrieve his coat and briefcase from the overhead luggage shelf.

There was no warning, no sudden braking, no whistle, just a lurching impact followed by another, and then stillness.

He told me that he remembers everything with crystal clarity. There was a young lady in the carriage with him who had so rushed to catch the train that she had not had time to purchase a ticket and therefore had written a cheque for the ticket inspector. 'I even remember who she banked with,' Peter said. 'It was Barclays.'

The guard came into the carriage saying that he did not know what had happened but his duty demanded that he place charges along the track behind the train to warn other trains.

This was the same technology that should have been utilised at Staplehurst and the same actions that should have been carried out in the Welwyn tunnel. As the guard left, Peter and the young lady discussed their options for escape and a sense of order and logic came over him, as it had come over Charles Dickens at Staplehurst. 'I knew we couldn't go forward so I told the lady that maybe we could head to the guard's van and exit at the rear of the train.' As they pondered their position, they saw a man outside the window completely blackened by fire. At this point they heard the doors of the carriage being unlocked and the voices of rescuers calling to them. They were helped out of the train and to ground level, which was a considerable drop when the train was not at a platform, and they made their way nervously across the rails, not knowing if the electrical current was still flowing through them. It was at this point that they glanced back at the wreckage and saw how lucky they had been. Towards the front of their train a raging fire burnt in one of the carriages sending columns of black smoke into the London sky.

Acting quickly the manager of a nearby branch of Sainsbury's supermarket closed its café to the public so that it could comfort and look after the confused and shocked survivors as they tried to make sense of what had happened to them, and here Peter and his new companion were joined by a third, a man wearing a light tanned jacket with diesel stains on it, and when they had become more calm the three stumbled into London to try and find a way home.

In the case of such a major disaster there was a protocol to shut down the underground system (in the moments after the crash it was not certain whether it had been the result of a terrorist attack), and as the trio tried to make their way into the

Tube a young police officer officiously said, 'You can't go down there, there's been a train crash this morning'. Peter, a well-mannered, polite man answered with an expletive, tersely pointing out that they were well aware there had been a crash as they had been in it!

Seeing their confusion, a passer-by riding a bicycle told them how to catch a bus to Victoria station where the companions, whose individual lives had never touched before that morning, and haven't touched again since, bade farewell to each other and went their separate ways. At Victoria Peter was able to board a bus home to Oxford.

He has little recollection of his journey home but remembers that once in Oxford he was completely confused, saying quietly, 'I didn't know where to go, I was completely disoriented, even though I know the city so well.' He had to be helped onto another bus to take him home. Over the next day or two the sheer shock of the experience overwhelmed him.

The symptoms that Peter experienced in the aftermath of Ladbroke Grove are astoundingly similar to those of Charles Dickens following Staplehurst. When travelling by train, which he had to do because of his job, there was a certain moment, a certain sound at a certain point on the line that caused him to start, to become nervous, to become 'aware' each time he passed it. Dickens experienced the same sort of thing when he felt the wheels of a train or cab rattle. As Peter's train thundered through the Oxfordshire countryside at speeds of over 100 mph, he felt nothing, but as the buildings of London encroached on the view, so his fears became more intense and the memories came back to him.

During our conversation there were times when the memory was too much, and Peter's eyes filled with tears as his voice faltered. At such moments he paused, breathed deeply, composed himself and then picked up the narrative just where he left it.

Such were the fears he experienced that his employers arranged for him to have the best counselling that money could buy, and eventually it became clear that the only short-term solution to Peter's condition was for him to change jobs and a few months after the crash he took up a new position in Oxfordshire that did not require him to travel into the city of London, through Ladbroke Grove.

As in the case of Charles Dickens, Peter's life continued, and the immediate shock passed and faded slightly until a completely unexpected trigger brought the memories to the surface once more. In Dickens' case it was the letter from Mark Lemon mentioning his involvement in a derailment. With Peter it was the terrible news footage on the 7th July in 2005 showing a London bus with its roof blown open by a terrorist bomb. 'Immediately the sight of the wreckage reminded me of Ladbroke Grove again. Not the death, not the bodies but the wreckage.' The bus was attacked in Tavistock Square at the site of Charles Dickens' London home, where he had first staged *The Frozen Deep*.

When Peter and I finished our conversation, we left his study and our respective moods lifted. He showed me his house and garden, and we discussed art and classical music. I felt honoured to have spoken to him about such a personal moment; a moment, he reflected, that changed his life forever and possibly for the better. But the sights he saw, the sounds he heard, the feelings he felt will stay with him forever, as they did with Charles Dickens.

THE FINAL JOURNEY

Charles Dickens had requested that he be buried somewhere near to his home at Gad's Hill Place, either in a simple village churchyard or within the precincts of Rochester Cathedral, such a central character in his unfinished mystery novel, but John Forster and Arthur Stanley, the Dean of Westminster Abbey, decreed that it would be a greater honour to a man who had touched the lives of so many if his final resting place were in Poet's Corner, and so it was with dreadful irony that the final journey of his earthly body was by train to Charing Cross station, where Warren's Blacking Factory had been situated and to where he himself had accompanied the gravely injured in the aftermath of the great Staplehurst disaster of 1865.

NO. 1 BRANCHLINE: THE SIGNALMAN by CHARLES DICKENS

'Halloa! Below there!'

When he heard a voice thus calling to him, he was standing at the door of his box, with a flag in his hand, furled round its short pole. One would have thought, considering the nature of the ground, that he could not have doubted from what quarter the voice came; but, instead of looking up to where I stood on the top of the steep cutting nearly over his head, he turned himself about and looked down the Line. There was something remarkable in his manner of doing so, though I could not have said, for my life, what. But I know it was remarkable enough to attract my notice, even though his figure was foreshortened and shadowed, down in the deep trench, and mine was high above him, so steeped in the glow of an angry sunset that I had shaded my eyes with my hand before I saw him at all.

'Halloa! Below!'

From looking down the Line, he turned himself about again, and, raising his eyes, saw my figure high above him.

'Is there any path by which I can come down and speak to you?'

He looked up at me without replying, and I looked down at him without pressing him too soon with a repetition of my idle question. Just then, there came a vague vibration in the earth and air, quickly changing into a violent pulsation, and an oncoming rush that caused me to start back, as though it had force to draw me down. When such vapour as rose to my height from this rapid train had passed me and was skimming away over the landscape, I looked down again, and saw him re-furling the flag he had shown while the train went by.

I repeated my inquiry. After a pause, during which he seemed to regard me with fixed attention, he motioned with his rolled-up flag towards a point on my level, some two or three hundred yards distant. I called down to him, 'All right!' and made for that point. There, by dint of looking closely about me, I found a rough zig-zag descending path notched out: which I followed.

The cutting was extremely deep, and unusually precipitate. It was made through a clammy stone that became oozier and wetter as I went down. For these reasons, I found the way long enough to give me time to recall a singular air of reluctance or compulsion with which he had pointed out the path.

When I came down low enough upon the zig-zag descent, to see him again, I saw that he was standing between the rails on the way by which the train had lately passed, in an attitude as if he were waiting for me to appear. He had his left hand at his chin, and that left elbow rested on his right hand crossed over his breast. His attitude was one of such expectation and watchfulness, that I stopped a moment, wondering at it.

I resumed my downward way, and, stepping out upon the level of the railroad and drawing nearer to him, saw that he was a dark sallow man, with a dark beard and rather heavy eyebrows. His post was in as solitary and dismal a place as ever I saw. On either side, a dripping-wet wall of jagged stone, excluding all view but a strip of sky; the perspective one way, only a crooked prolongation of this great dungeon; the shorter perspective in the other direction, terminating in a gloomy red light, and the gloomier entrance to a black tunnel, in whose massive architecture there was a barbarous, depressing, and forbidding air. So little sunlight ever found its way to this spot that it had an earthy deadly smell; and so much cold wind rushed through it that it struck chill to me, as if I had left the natural world.

Before he stirred, I was near enough to him to have touched him. Not even then removing his eyes from mine, he stepped back one step, and lifted his hand.

This was a lonesome post to occupy (I said), and it had riveted my attention when I looked down from up yonder. A visitor was a rarity, I should suppose; not an unwelcome rarity, I hoped? In me, he merely saw a man who had been shut up within narrow limits all his life, and who, being at last set free, had a newly awakened interest in these great works. To such purpose I spoke to him; but I am far from sure of the terms I used, for, besides that I am not happy in opening any conversation, there was something in the man that daunted me.

He directed a most curious look towards the red light near the tunnel's mouth, and looked all about it, as if something were missing from it, and then looked at me.

That light was part of his charge? Was it not?

He answered in a low voice: 'Don't you know it is?'

The monstrous thought came into my mind as I perused the fixed eyes and the saturnine face, that this was a spirit, not a man. I have speculated since, whether there may have been infection in his mind.

In my turn, I stepped back. But in making the action, I detected in his eyes some latent fear of me. This put the monstrous thought to flight.

'You look at me,' I said, forcing a smile, 'as if you had a dread of me.'

'I was doubtful,' he returned, 'whether I had seen you before.'

'Where?'

He pointed to the red light he had looked at.

'There?' I said.

Intently watchful of me, he replied (but without sound), Yes.

'My good fellow, what should I do there? However, be that as it may, I never was there, you may swear.'

'I think I may,' he re-joined. 'Yes. I am sure I may.'

His manner cleared, like my own. He replied to my remarks with readiness, and in well-chosen words. Had he much to do there? Yes; that was to say, he had enough responsibility to bear; but exactness and watchfulness were what was required of him, and of actual work — manual labour — he had next to none. To change that signal, to trim those lights, and to turn this iron handle now and then, was all he had to do under that head. Regarding those many long and lonely hours of which I seemed to make so much, he could only say that the routine of his life had shaped itself into that form, and he had grown used to it. He had taught himself a language down here — if only to know it by sight, and to have formed his own crude ideas of its pronunciation, could be called learning it. He had also worked at fractions and decimals, and tried a little algebra; but he was, and had been as a boy, a poor hand at figures. Was it necessary for him when on duty, always to remain in that channel of damp air, and could he never rise into the sunshine from between those high stone walls? Why, that depended upon times and circumstances. Under some conditions there would be less upon the Line than under others, and the same held good as to certain hours of the day and night. In bright weather, he did choose occasions for getting a little above these lower shadows; but, being at all times liable to be called by his electric bell, and at such times listening for it with redoubled anxiety, the relief was less than I would suppose.

He took me into his box, where there was a fire, a desk for an official book in which he had to make certain entries, a telegraphic instrument with its dial face and needles, and the little bell of which he had spoken. On my trusting that he would excuse the remark that he had been well-educated, and (I hoped I might say without offence), perhaps educated above that station, he observed that instances of slight incongruity in such-wise would rarely be found wanting among large bodies of men; that he had heard it was so in workhouses, in the police force, even in that last desperate resource, the army; and that he knew it was so, more or less, in any great railway staff. He had been, when young (if I could believe it, sitting in that hut; he scarcely could), a student of natural philosophy, and had attended lectures; but he had run wild, misused his opportunities, gone down, and never risen again. He had no complaint to offer about that. He had made his bed and he lay upon it. It was far too late to make another.

All that I have here condensed, he said in a quiet manner, with his grave dark regards divided between me and the fire. He threw in the word 'sir' from time to time, and especially when he referred to his youth: as though to request me to understand that he claimed to be nothing but what I found him. He was several times interrupted by the little bell, and had to read off messages, and send replies. Once, he had to stand without the door, and display a flag as a train passed, and make some verbal communication to the driver. In the discharge of his duties I observed him to be remarkably exact and vigilant, breaking off his discourse at a syllable, and remaining silent until what he had to do was done.

In a word, I should have set this man down as one of the safest of men to be employed in that capacity, but for the circumstance that while he was speaking to me he twice broke off with a fallen colour, turned his face towards the little bell when it did NOT ring, opened the door of the hut (which was kept shut to exclude the unhealthy damp), and looked out towards the red light near the mouth of the tunnel. On both of those occasions, he came back to the fire with the inexplicable air upon him which I had remarked, without being able to define, when we were so far asunder.

Said I when I rose to leave him: 'You almost make me think that I have met with a contented man.' (I am afraid I must acknowledge that I said it to lead him on.)

'I believe I used to be so,' he re-joined, in the low voice in which he had first spoken; 'but I am troubled, sir, I am troubled.'

He would have recalled the words if he could. He had said them, however, and I took them up quickly.

'With what? What is your trouble?'

'It is very difficult to impart, sir. It is very, very difficult to speak of. If ever you make me another visit, I will try to tell you.'

'But I expressly intend to make you another visit. Say, when shall it be?'

'I go off early in the morning, and I shall be on again at ten to-morrow night, sir.'

'I will come at eleven.'

He thanked me and went out at the door with me.

'I'll show my white light, sir,' he said, in his peculiar low voice, 'till you have found the way up. When you have found it, don't call out! And when you are at the top, don't call out!'

His manner seemed to make the place strike colder to me, but I said no more than, 'Very well.'

'And when you come down to-morrow night, don't call out! Let me ask you a parting question. What made you cry "Halloa! Below there!" to-night?'

'Heaven knows,' said I, 'I cried something to that effect—'

'Not to that effect, sir. Those were the very words. I know them well.'

'Admit those were the very words. I said them, no doubt, because I saw you below.'

'For no other reason?'

'What other reason could I possibly have!'

'You had no feeling that they were conveyed to you in any supernatural way?'

'No.'

He wished me good night and held up his light. I walked by the side of the down Line of rails (with a very disagreeable sensation of a train coming behind me), until I found the path. It was easier to mount than to descend, and I got back to my inn without any adventure.

Punctual to my appointment, I placed my foot on the first notch of the zig-zag next night, as the distant clocks were striking eleven. He was waiting for me at the bottom, with his white light on. 'I have not called out,' I said, when we came close together; 'may I speak now?'

'By all means, sir.'

'Good night then, and here's my hand.'

'Good night, sir, and here's mine.' With that, we walked side by side to his box, entered it, closed the door, and sat down by the fire.

'I have made up my mind, sir,' he began, bending forward as soon as we were seated, and speaking in a tone but a little above a whisper, 'that you shall not have to ask me twice what troubles me. I took you for someone else yesterday evening. That troubles me.'

'That mistake?'

'No. That someone else.'

'Who is it?'

'I don't know.'

'Like me?'

'I don't know. I never saw the face. The left arm is across the face, and the right arm is waved. Violently waved. This way.'

I followed his action with my eyes, and it was the action of an arm gesticulating with the utmost passion and vehemence: 'For God's sake clear the way!'

'One moonlight night,' said the man, 'I was sitting here, when I heard a voice cry "Halloa! Below there!" I started up, looked from that door, and saw this Someone else standing by the red light near the tunnel, waving as I just now showed you. The voice seemed hoarse with shouting, and it cried, "Look out! Look out!" And then again "Halloa! Below there! Look out!" I caught up my lamp, turned it on red, and ran towards the figure, calling, "What's wrong? What has happened? Where?" It stood just outside the blackness of the tunnel. I advanced so close upon it that I wondered at its keeping the sleeve across its eyes. I ran right up at it, and had my hand stretched out to pull the sleeve away, when it was gone.'

'Into the tunnel,' said I.

'No. I ran on into the tunnel, five hundred yards. I stopped and held my lamp above my head, and saw the figures of the measured distance, and saw the wet stains stealing down the walls and trickling through the arch. I ran out again, faster than I had run in (for I had a mortal abhorrence of the place upon me), and I looked all-round the red light with my own red light, and I went up the iron ladder to the gallery atop of it, and I came down again, and ran back here. I telegraphed both ways, "An alarm has been given. Is anything wrong?" The answer came back, both ways: "All well."'

Resisting the slow touch of a frozen finger tracing out my spine, I showed him how that this figure must be a deception of his sense of sight, and how that figures, originating in disease of the delicate nerves that minister to the functions of the eye, were known to have often troubled patients, some of whom had become conscious of the nature of their affliction, and had even proved it by experiments upon themselves. 'As to an imaginary cry,' said I, 'do but listen for a moment to the wind in this unnatural valley while we speak so low, and to the wild harp it makes of the telegraph wires!'

That was all very well, he returned, after we had sat listening for a while, and he ought to know something of the wind and the wires, he who so often passed long winter nights there, alone and watching. But he would beg to remark that he had not finished.

I asked his pardon, and he slowly added these words, touching my arm: 'Within six hours after the Appearance, the memorable accident on this Line happened, and within ten hours the dead and wounded were brought along through the tunnel over the spot where the figure had stood.'

A disagreeable shudder crept over me, but I did my best against it. It was not to be denied, I re-joined, that this was a remarkable coincidence, calculated deeply to impress his mind. But it was unquestionable that remarkable coincidences did continually occur, and they must be taken into account in dealing with such a subject. Though to be sure I must admit, I added (for I thought I saw that he was going to bring the objection to bear upon me), men of common sense did not allow much for coincidences in making the ordinary calculations of life.

He again begged to remark that he had not finished.

I again begged his pardon for being betrayed into interruptions.

'This,' he said, again laying his hand upon my arm, and glancing over his shoulder with hollow eyes, 'was just a year ago. Six or seven months passed, and I had recovered from the surprise and shock, when one morning, as the day was breaking, I, standing at that door, looked towards the red light, and saw the spectre again.' He stopped, with a fixed look at me.

'Did it cry out?'
'No. It was silent.'

'Did it wave its arm?'

'No. It leaned against the shaft of the light, with both hands before the face. Like this.'

Once more, I followed his action with my eyes. It was an action of mourning. I have seen such an attitude in stone figures on tombs.

'Did you go up to it?'

'I came in and sat down, partly to collect my thoughts, partly because it had turned me faint. When I went to the door again, daylight was above me, and the ghost was gone.'

'But nothing followed? Nothing came of this?'

He touched me on the arm with his forefinger twice or thrice, giving a ghastly nod each time: 'That very day, as a train came out of the tunnel, I noticed, at a carriage window on my side, what looked like a confusion of hands and heads, and something waved. I saw it, just in time to signal the driver, Stop! He shut off, and put his brake on, but the train drifted past here a hundred and fifty yards or more. I ran after it, and, as I went along, heard terrible screams and cries. A beautiful young lady had died instantaneously in one of the compartments, and was brought in here, and laid down on this floor between us.'

Involuntarily, I pushed my chair back, as I looked from the boards at which he pointed, to himself. 'True, sir. True. Precisely as it happened, so I tell it you.'

I could think of nothing to say, to any purpose, and my mouth was very dry. The wind and the wires took up the story with a long lamenting wail.

He resumed. 'Now, sir, mark this, and judge how my mind is troubled. The spectre came back, a week ago. Ever since, it has been there, now and again, by fits and starts.'

'At the light?'

'At the Danger-light.'

'What does it seem to do?'

He repeated, if possible, with increased passion and vehemence, that former gesticulation of: 'For God's sake clear the way!'

Then, he went on. 'I have no peace or rest for it. It calls to me, for many minutes together, in an agonised manner, "Below there! Look out! Look out!" It stands waving to me. It rings my little bell—'

I caught at that. 'Did it ring your bell yesterday evening when I was here, and you went to the door?'

'Twice.'

'Why, see,' said I, 'how your imagination misleads you. My eyes were on the bell, and my ears were open to the bell, and if I am a living man, it did NOT ring at those times. No, nor at any other time, except when it was rung in the natural course of physical things by the station communicating with you.'

He shook his head. 'I have never made a mistake as to that, yet, sir. I have never confused the spectre's ring with the man's. The ghost's ring is a strange vibration in the bell that it derives from nothing else, and I have not asserted that the bell stirs to the eye. I don't wonder that you failed to hear it. But I heard it.'

'And did the spectre seem to be there, when you looked out?'

'It WAS there.'

'Both times?'

He repeated firmly: 'Both times.'

'Will you come to the door with me, and look for it now?'

He bit his under-lip as though he were somewhat unwilling but arose. I opened the door, and stood on the step, while he stood in the doorway. There, was the Danger-light. There, was the dismal mouth of the tunnel. There, were the high wet stone walls of the cutting. There, were the stars above them.

'Do you see it?' I asked him, taking particular note of his face. His eyes were prominent and strained; but not very much more so, perhaps, than my own had been when I had directed them earnestly towards the same spot.

'No,' he answered. 'It is not there.'

'Agreed,' said I.

We went in again, shut the door, and resumed our seats. I was thinking how best to improve this advantage, if it might be called one, when he took up the conversation in such a matter of course way, so assuming that there could be no serious question of fact between us, that I felt myself placed in the weakest of positions.

'By this time, you will fully understand, sir,' he said, 'that what troubles me so dreadfully, is the question, what does the spectre mean?'

I was not sure, I told him, that I did fully understand.

'What is its warning against?' he said, ruminating, with his eyes on the fire, and only by times turning them on me. 'What is the danger? Where is the danger? There is danger overhanging, somewhere on the Line. Some dreadful calamity will happen. It is not to be doubted this third time, after what has gone before. But surely this is a cruel haunting of me. What can I do?'

He pulled out his handkerchief and wiped the drops from

his heated forehead.

'If I telegraph Danger, on either side of me, or on both, I can give no reason for it,' he went on, wiping the palms of his hands. 'I should get into trouble and do no good. They would think I was mad. This is the way it would work: — Message: "Danger! Take care!" Answer: "What danger? Where?" Message: "Don't know. But for God's sake take care!" They would displace me. What else could they do?'

His pain of mind was most pitiable to see. It was the mental torture of a conscientious man, oppressed beyond endurance by an unintelligible responsibility involving life.

'When it first stood under the Danger-light,' he went on, putting his dark hair back from his head, and drawing his hands outward across and across his temples in an extremity of feverish distress, 'why not tell me where that accident was to happen — if it must happen? Why not tell me how it could be averted — if it could have been averted? When on its second coming it hid its face, why not tell me instead: "She is going to die. Let them keep her at home"? If it came, on those two occasions, only to show me that its warnings were true, and so to prepare me for the third, why not warn me plainly now? And I, Lord help me! A mere poor signalman on this solitary station! Why not go to somebody with credit to be believed, and power to act!'

When I saw him in this state, I saw that for the poor man's sake, as well as for the public safety, what I had to do for the time was to compose his mind. Therefore, setting aside all question of reality or unreality between us, I represented to him that whoever thoroughly discharged his duty, must do well, and that at least it was his comfort that he understood his duty, though he did not understand these confounding

Appearances. In this effort I succeeded far better than in the attempt to reason him out of his conviction. He became calm; the occupations incidental to his post as the night advanced, began to make larger demands on his attention; and I left him at two in the morning. I had offered to stay through the night, but he would not hear of it.

That I more than once looked back at the red light as I ascended the pathway, that I did not like the red light, and that I should have slept but poorly if my bed had been under it, I see no reason to conceal. Nor, did I like the two sequences of the accident and the dead girl. I see no reason to conceal that, either.

But what ran most in my thoughts was the consideration how ought I to act, having become the recipient of this disclosure? I had proved the man to be intelligent, vigilant, painstaking, and exact; but how long might he remain so, in his state of mind? Though in a subordinate position, still he held a most important trust, and would I (for instance) like to stake my own life on the chances of his continuing to execute it with precision?

Unable to overcome a feeling that there would be something treacherous in my communicating what he had told me, to his superiors in the Company, without first being plain with himself and proposing a middle course to him, I ultimately resolved to offer to accompany him (otherwise keeping his secret for the present) to the wisest medical practitioner we could hear of in those parts, and to take his opinion. A change in his time of duty would come round next night, he had apprised me, and he would be off an hour or two after sunrise, and on again soon after sunset. I had appointed to return accordingly.

Next evening was a lovely evening, and I walked out early

to enjoy it. The sun was not yet quite down when I traversed the field-path near the top of the deep cutting. I would extend my walk for an hour, I said to myself, half an hour on and half an hour back, and it would then be time to go to my signalman's box.

Before pursuing my stroll, I stepped to the brink, and mechanically looked down, from the point from which I had first seen him. I cannot describe the thrill that seized upon me, when, close at the mouth of the tunnel, I saw the appearance of a man, with his left sleeve across his eyes, passionately waving his right arm.

The nameless horror that oppressed me passed in a moment, for in a moment I saw that this appearance of a man was a man indeed, and that there was a little group of other men standing at a short distance, to whom he seemed to be rehearsing the gesture he made. The Danger-light was not yet lighted. Against its shaft, a little low hut, entirely new to me, had been made of some wooden supports and tarpaulin. It looked no bigger than a bed.

With an irresistible sense that something was wrong — with a flashing self-reproachful fear that fatal mischief had come of my leaving the man there, and causing no one to be sent to overlook or correct what he did — I descended the notched path with all the speed I could make.

'What is the matter?' I asked the men.

'Signalman killed this morning, sir.'

'Not the man belonging to that box?'

'Yes, sir.'

'Not the man I know?'

'You will recognise him, sir, if you knew him,' said the man who spoke for the others, solemnly uncovering his own head and raising an end of the tarpaulin, 'for his face is quite composed.'

'O! How did this happen, how did this happen?' I asked, turning from one to another as the hut closed in again.

'He was cut down by an engine, sir. No man in England knew his work better. But somehow, he was not clear of the outer rail. It was just at broad day. He had struck the light and had the lamp in his hand. As the engine came out of the tunnel, his back was towards her, and she cut him down. That man drove her and was showing how it happened. Show the gentleman, Tom.'

The man, who wore a rough dark dress, stepped back to his former place at the mouth of the tunnel!

'Coming round the curve in the tunnel, sir,' he said, 'I saw him at the end, like as if I saw him down a perspective-glass. There was no time to check speed, and I knew him to be very careful. As he didn't seem to take heed of the whistle, I shut it off when we were running down upon him and called to him as loud as I could call.'

'What did you say?'

'I said, "Below there! Look out! Look out! For God's sake clear the way!"'

I started.

'Ah! it was a dreadful time, sir. I never left off calling to him. I put this arm before my eyes, not to see, and I waved this arm to the last; but it was no use.'

Without prolonging the narrative to dwell on any one of its curious circumstances more than on any other, I may, in closing it, point out the coincidence that the warning of the engine driver included, not only the words which the unfortunate signalman had repeated to me as haunting him, but also the words which I myself — not he — had attached, and that only in my own mind, to the gesticulation he had imitated.

Illustration Credits:

Page 11 **Rail embankment at Staplehurst.** Author
Page 19: **Charles Dickens with his dog Turk:** Charles Dickens Museum
Page 35: **Young Dickens posting manuscript:** Charles Dickens Museum
Page 51: **Interior Free Trade Hall, Manchester**
Page 70: **Paris Gare du Nord:**
Page 73: **Hop pickers**
Page 78: **Manet, The Folkestone Boat**: Philadelphia Museum of Art: The Mr. and Mrs. Carroll S. Tyson, Jr., Collection, 1963, 1963-116-10
P 85: **Quay railway station:** 4Fi1158 ©Archives Boulogne-sur-Mer
P 87: **Boat at quayside:** 61Fi383©Archives Boulogne-sur-Mer
Page 88: **The Victoria steamer**
Page 97: **Railway map South Eastern Railway Company routes**
Page 99: **Albion Villas Folkestone.** Author
Page 102: **Folkestone Harbour**
Page 104: **222 Dover Mail Single locomotive**
Page 121: **Engraving of crash site**: Charles Dickens Museum
Page 128: **Photo montage of crash site:** Charles Dickens Museum
Page 133: **The Penny Illustrated cover:** Charles Dickens Museum
Page 146: **The Staplehurst Railway Hotel today:** Author
Page 177: **Frederick Bodenham:** Herefordshire Archive Service
Page 185: **Clayton Tunnel**
Page 189: **Charles Dickens in New York:** Charles Dickens Museum
Page 191: **Performing Sikes and Nancy:** Charles Dickens Museum
Page 203: **The Empty Chair:** Charles Dickens Museum
Page 214: **Charles Dickens's grave**: Charles Dickens Museum
Page 237: **Author performing The Signalman**

CPSIA information can be obtained
at www.ICGtesting.com
Printed in the USA
FSHW012316021221
86650FS